BORN TO BE DIFFERENT

By

Betty Fotheringham

Best wishes

Betty

ISBN: - 13: 978 – 1499110562

10: 1499110561

This book is dedicated to my late husband Frank, my biggest supporter who always "knew" I could write a book.

My good friend Bob, but for you my healing journey may never have begun.

My birth mother Betty who, however reluctantly, gave me the precious gift of life. You kept your side of our "deal", I hope I have kept mine.

Acknowledgments

My grateful thanks go first to my family. It must have been difficult at times to have a mum who was so "different".

And to all those who came for healing, all my students, the writers of all the books I have studied and so enjoyed, all my teachers, seen and unseen and all others who have journeyed with me through this life. You have all taught me so much.

CONTENTS

INTRODUCTION

Well here it is! All those of you who have encouraged me to get down to finishing this second book, I really hope you enjoy it. It's a wander through my "different" life, of at first being terrified of ghosts or spirits, to coming to terms with them and finally understanding what they, and pretty much what the whole of my life has been about. In this book I tell of spirit people, my pathetic attempt at mediumship, of spiritual healing, reincarnation and so much more. I even give my definition of God. How risky is that then? Please read with an open mind. What I have to say may just all be true! Then where would you be? Some names have been changed for the sake of privacy, as I appreciate not everyone may wish to be mentioned as being part of my spooky world. For those who wanted to hear of how my unfortunate circumstances of birth affected my later life, I have written the last chapter especially for you.

On a serious note nothing in this book is meant to take the place of proper medical diagnosis and attention. If you feel you need to see your doctor. Do it! Don't be daft about that.

And now — off you go — read away

CHAPTER 1

A SPOOKY WELCOME!

I was sixteen, going on seventeen, when I had my first real spooky experience. This was 1949/50 and I still have a very clear picture in my memory of how this came about. It wasn't something I was likely to forget in a hurry. My boyfriend Frank wanted me to meet his parents before we announced our engagement. They lived on the outskirts of Elgin in the north east of Scotland. My future father-in-law was the superintendent of Alexander's buses for that area and their house was next to the depot. I lived with my adoptive parents on a small croft just north of Stonehaven. (I told of my rough and ready life on the croft in my first book "The Crofter Quine.") I arrived in Elgin having had what at that time, was a very long journey, by bus of course, with no dual carriageways and no toilets on the way. To add to my discomfort I was a very poor traveller and on arrival, not only did I desperately need the loo, but I was also trying very hard not to be sick. Buses do that to me anyway, but I was

Betty Fotheringham

also very nervous about meeting my future in-laws. With Stonehaven being such a small town I had heard a little about them and I wasn't too sure that Frank's mother was going to like me. It seemed she had a reputation for being a bit uppity. People were very judgmental at that time, sometimes unfairly.

After the introductions were over I asked if I might use the bathroom. I quickly locked the door, dashed over to the loo with hardly a glance around, sat down and pee'd all over the lid. Toilets on crofts didn't have lids you see, so this was a new one on me. I could see I was going to have to up my game a bit. At least I forgot to be sick. Now this would not have been how I would have chosen to start my visit to my prospective in-laws and sadly it was all downhill thereafter.

I was given the best bedroom upstairs to the front of the house. It has always seemed to me a very silly custom of that time to allocate the best room in the house to the occasional visitor. At home on our croft this applied too. Our best room was furnished as a bedsit. Rarely did anyone sleep there and nor was the "sitting" part used much either. It was kept tidy in case the minister dropped by but this didn't happen often for ministers didn't always own a car, and a three mile journey from the town into the country (usually by bicycle) probably didn't appeal to them much. On the odd occasion when it did, it would have been to persuade us to attend Communion. The minister was no fool and would know that Sundays on crofts were our busiest days, so a weekly church attendance just wouldn't happen. Our souls could just be saved though if we came to Communion twice a year, or so we were told.

The minister's visit was greatly dreaded and when he did drop by I would be sent scurrying to the dresser to find saucers to match cups. I would blow the dust off them and then Mum would give them a wipe with the corner of her apron. She always wore two aprons, the top one for grubby tasks, the one underneath always freshly laundered. The top one would be whisked off if an unexpected visitor dropped by. The minister was then presented with his cup of tea and a homemade something or other. What a fuss if the baking tins were empty and he had to make do with a bought biscuit. Serving bought biscuits to visitors at that time was a loss of face and to be avoided at all costs. All this was accompanied by normal conversation on the minister's side and my Mum using her very posh voice kept for such occasions. Since she didn't get a lot of practice there was usually a broad Scots word thrown in when she got stuck for the English equivalent.

(Now if you are wondering when I am going to get to the spooky bit just hang on in there I won't be long now and yes, I know I do go on a bit.)

So with this attitude to the best room in a house and everything in the bedroom at Frank's parents' house being new, (they had only recently moved there) I found it very daunting. I tiptoed around in it as being part of the Smith family new anything was strange to me. We only did new when every other means of acquiring what we needed had been explored. Furniture came from roups and in a croft house carpets were unheard of. Rugs we did have, (mostly rag rugs handmade in the winter to pass the time) but we never had a carpet. Frank's Mum and Dad had the bedroom next to mine to the back of the house, his brother Laurie was across the landing and downstairs in the sitting room there was a bed settee shared by Frank and his brother Ian, who also happened to be visiting for the weekend, possibly to give me the onceover, and who could blame him.

Sadly my future parents-in-law were stiff and formal on my arrival at their home, and subsequent events didn't improve this situation. It must be remembered that meeting prospective daughters in law was as new to them as my situation of meeting future in laws, and perhaps I too was not at my most relaxed. But it did seem that news of my illegitimacy had gone before me and this had a bit to do with my welcome and maybe too, acceptance as a suitable person to marry their eldest son was never going to happen anyway. I have to be realistic, parents always want the best for their family and a crofter's daughter wasn't much of a catch. However the event of that first night under their roof sealed my fate as an unacceptable prospective daughter-in-law.

Later when I retired to my posh bedroom I still felt very vulnerable and nervous and I prayed I wouldn't wet the bed. The odds on this occurring were very slim indeed, but it was something that had happened to me once when I was about four years old and staying with my brother Wullie and his wife Violet in their home in Gourdon. Socially unacceptable as this "accident" was in itself, it was made doubly so when I tell you that I was sharing *their* bed at the time. Now you can appreciate why this past memory preyed on my mind a bit and I hadn't been away from home since that time. We Smiths just didn't get about much, hence the loo lid incident.

I had no trouble getting to sleep that night though, as I found the air in that part of the country so soporific that I could have slept on the edge of a spade, as the old saying goes. Later that night I woke from a deep sleep, (no I was *not* dreaming) and there standing by my side was a very old man. I saw him quite clearly. His dress was from a much earlier age and he wore a very serious expression on his face. One arm was extended towards me and in this hand he held a book. I didn't take time to consider that perhaps he was *giving* me this book, I thought he was about to hit me with it! I screamed over and over again. At the first sound I made he vanished – he just faded out. Who could blame him? I continued screaming and downstairs Frank and Ian shot out of bed. Ian was convinced that

11

some poor girl was being assaulted on the road outside and with much banging of doors headed in that direction. Now Ian, at that time, had quite a mop of unruly black curls and wearing only his pyjamas, if there had indeed been a damsel in distress, she might very well have considered that my future brother in law presented an equally challenging sight. Frank on the other hand took the stairs two at a time and burst into my room where I was now sobbing hysterically.

The true story of what I experienced could not be told. I wasn't going to be labelled off my head as well as being socially inferior, so I said I'd had a bad dream. Frank accepted this without question and in a little while peace reigned in the house once more. During all this his parents never stirred, nor did they make any comment in the morning. It was as if the incident had never happened. Would it have been possible for me to make a worse impression on my future in-laws I wonder?

That experience, being the first of its kind, terrified me for a very long time. I so wanted to believe it had been a bad dream, but deep down I knew this was not so. Up until then I had little knowledge of spirit people. My mother had a tale of when she and her sister were young and they too saw a ghost as they called her. This story goes that a friend from a little way down the road (they lived in the country somewhere around Ellon in Aberdeenshire) had dropped by for a wee while one winter's evening and my mother, her sister and the family dog were seeing her part of the way home. This was a very common practice at that time amongst country folk.

On this occasion they had only travelled a little way when, in front of them, appeared a woman they had never seen before. They stopped in great surprise and a bit of fear for none of them had seen this figure approaching. The road was empty one minute and then there she was a few yards from them. As soon as they were aware of her presence (and they all saw her quite clearly) she vanished. As with my night-time visitor there was no walking away, just a fading out. Now my mother said that given time, they might have persuaded themselves that what they had witnessed was imagination, albeit surprising that the three of them could describe this person in exactly the same words, had it not been for the behaviour of their dog. It had stopped suddenly in the middle of the road in front of the woman, gave a yelp, then turned round and raced for home. That dog never went near that bit of road again. From that night on it would turn just short of that spot and return home on its own. After that experience my mother believed in "ghosts" and so my mind was open to accepting that my experience too had been real.

Little did I imagine then as a teenager how my life would change, and in the years to come how I would eventually be able to communicate with spirit people, become a spiritual healer and tutor, and how all this would change me and my understanding of the meaning of life.

CHAPTER 2

BECOMING MORE AWARE

Frank and I were duly married in Stonehaven just before my nineteenth birthday. With the excitement of getting engaged and planning my wedding I found it easy to put the ghostly Elgin incident to the back of my mind. I really believed it to be a one off. If only. But I was now to be living in Edinburgh away from the countryside for the first time in my life and this move was exciting and at the same time scary. I had quite a bit of adjusting to do as I quickly found that until then, I had been living in a very trusting environment indeed, where almost everyone knew my father, Wullie Smith, and where neighbours all knew and helped each other. For instance, I was now being told by my new husband that I must never accept lifts from strangers. What a fuss just because one day when a car had stopped beside me at a bus stop in Corstorphine, I had hopped into the front seat beside a rather astonished driver. This man had stopped, he quickly told me, because he had mistaken me for someone else. I then got a sound talking to on what not to do in a city. I was subsequently dropped off at

15

my office door in the West End after I had promised him I would never get into a stranger's car again. Now wasn't that kind of him and wasn't I lucky that day? To be fair to myself, living in the country, we would never have dreamt of refusing a lift from anyone. That would have seemed ungrateful, and if you had three miles to walk in the pouring rain, accepting a lift from a passerby seemed like the sensible thing to do.

On another occasion Frank pointed out to me that being offered a modelling job by someone on a bus was almost certainly not what it seemed, and was unlikely to lead to a worthwhile career. I was sure it would beat secretarial work any day and I rather fancied myself as a model. What nineteen year-old wouldn't? Another lesson to learn and remember. This new life was turning out to be quite a contrast to my old one. I obviously still had much to learn.

Back on the croft at that time we lived by the seasons and respected Mother Nature and her ways. We could smell snow, sense a thunder storm long before it arrived, and we watched the behaviour of the birds and animals for other signs of any change in the weather. In a dry summer we dowsed for extra sources of water for the animals. We rarely needed a vet for them as my mother had various remedies which she concocted from the leaves or roots of certain plants, and my father certainly knew a thing or two about other problems befalling any animal. He was particularly knowledgeable about horses as he had worked with them most of his farm servant life. As for our own health, as there was no National Health Service at that time, doctors had to be paid and with little money to spare for this it was fortunate that we were rarely ill. In the unlikely event of one of us being under the weather, self-treating with natural remedies was our way, and I only realized years later how very suitable and supportive a background this was for me in what was to become my long career as a healer and tutor.

We were very open to "sensing" what was around us, but this was rarely discussed because it was accepted as normal. Why would we discuss a natural ability that we all possessed? Occasionally mention would be made of certain people we knew who were particularly gifted in this way and who just seemed to know things. They were held in high regard and their advice would be sought on occasions and always trusted.

After marrying I left the familiarity of that life behind and found myself living in the city, in a world of strangers of such mixed backgrounds. It seems hardly believable that up to that point in my life I probably hadn't seen more than half a dozen people of a different nationality to my own.

In spite of this change in my lifestyle I settled down with only a few strange happenings around me. The first flat we lived in had a very uncomfortable feel to it. It was at the top of an old house in Stockbridge and I was always sure when there alone, that previous long gone tenants came visiting to give me the once over. I never actually saw any spirit people but I could sense them around me. They did always seem friendly so I assumed that they approved of me. But friendly or not after the Elgin incident I felt quite uncomfortable with this. At that time Frank worked on one of the daily newspapers and, depending on his work hours, I was alone most nights. This in itself was a small challenge for, up until then, I had never spent a night alone in any house. But hey, I was a married woman now, living in a big city and I could cope with a few unseen spirit beings and perhaps they were only in my imagination. As long as I couldn't see them I could half believe that. How easily the mind can deceive. We see what we want to see and believe what we want to believe.

That first year we changed flats every few months. We were trying to save enough money for a deposit on a house of our own and our flats got smaller and cheaper until we finally moved into a large bedsit in Brandon Street with shared kitchen and bathroom. Now we could really save. I quickly made friends with the occupant of the next room, and felt that I could settle and be happy in my new surroundings until we could achieve our dream of buying our own home. Perhaps I was counting my chickens a little prematurely for very soon my new friend told me the big "secret" of this house. The owner lived with her daughter downstairs in the garden flat and it seemed they were both spiritualists. Now spiritualism was not a religion that I knew anything about. We had simply never heard of it in Stonehaven. From this base of complete ignorance I formed the opinion that I didn't like it. Just how judgmental was that then?

Worse was to come. Spiritualist meetings were held every Tuesday evening in the room directly below ours. Now this was a terrifying thought for me. I considered that I was on the direct flight path of visiting spirits, assuming that they came straight down from heaven or wherever they hung out, to this flat below me. The first Tuesday after this, I got home from work, (Frank had already left) I had a quick snack and shot off to the nearest cinema. I wasn't hanging about waiting for any spirits passing through our room. I had a clear memory still of my first encounter.

After a few weeks I was brave enough to stay in on Tuesday evenings and although still a little uncomfortable with the idea of a séance (whatever form that took) taking place in the room below me, I came to realise that spiritualists were thoroughly nice normal people and not once did I bump into any spirit beings making their way to or from the meetings. I didn't even sense their presence. Maybe they used the front door like the rest of us.

Here though was this other world I was reluctantly learning about and maybe it wasn't such a scary one as I had imagined, but I still wanted nothing to do with it and I certainly didn't want to discuss the subject with anyone.

Frank and I moved into our own home in Corstorphine a year after our marriage and that was heaven. A heaven with little in the way of furniture, electrical gadgets or other "necessities" but most of what we did have was new and we were happy. When it came to decorating our home, for the first time in my life I realised that not all doors and windows had to be green or brown, and walls did not have to be cream, nor ceilings white. I could actually choose *bright* colours! This would have caused a right speak on a croft I can tell you. It would have been considered that you were getting a bittie above yourself to break with tradition. To be fair there was so much work to be done on a croft that there was very little time for decorating, and inside painting or papering was usually left to the women. Paint and wallpapers were almost impossible to get during the Second World War and were snapped up at roups. Now I was able to choose anything that took my fancy. I started off with a colour scheme of bright turquoise and coral for our new hall.

No more lobbies for me, I now had a hall like other townsers. From early childhood and with me living in the country I always wanted to be a townser. It was the old story of the grass being greener. Now I do appreciate that the bright colours I chose then are nothing compared to today, but during and for a time after the Second World War, our world was a distinctly grey place and my choice was considered very garish indeed.

Many years on I trained in the psychology and therapeutic use of colour. Even the excitement I felt over that could not dim the memory of that early excitement I found in experimenting with the bright colours in every room of our first home. This deep love of colour has stayed with me all my life. I had other discoveries though waiting for me. It was as if my whole life was opening in different directions all at once and I couldn't wait.

My first job after getting married, was in a chartered accountant's office in the West End overlooking a large craft shop. My lunch times were spent poring over all the bits and pieces that, when put together, produced beautiful things. Here was yet another untouched world for me. Apart from the rag rugs we made on the croft and the bits of sewing I did for my bottom drawer, I had never seen anything like this. I fell in love with the pretty stones for jewellery making and taught myself this craft, quickly followed by many others. In a very short time I had come a long way from my school handwork classes.

During the Second World War years I was at the Mackie Academy in Stonehaven where the teachers tried to improve my education. I was not academically clever and I didn't fare much better in the handwork classes either. One day because of the war, we were all told we had to knit jerseys for refugees. My only experience of these poor children had been at my previous school at Catterline and it wasn't a happy one. They had given me head lice and I was never going to forgive that. So why would I want to knit jerseys for them? (*There is a reason for telling you this tale so please stay with me.*) I never did finish knitting that refugee jersey and as I was holding up the dispatch of the school's consignment the teacher asked another girl to finish it for me. Very unfairly, I felt huge resentment towards this poor girl. Now come forward in time with me by some sixty odd years. I happened to be in Aberdeen one evening giving a talk on embroidery to a large gathering. (Yes my creative skills did improve.) When the talk was over I saw a smartly dressed lady approaching me from the audience. Immediately I felt a strong resentment towards her and this I could not understand. Why should I feel like this towards a complete stranger? She introduced herself (the name meant nothing to me) and then reminded me that we had been at school together. Instantly I knew who she was and why I felt this strong resentment. I blurted out, quite sharply I may say, "*You* finished knitting my refugee jersey!" We laughed about it together but nevertheless that strong antagonistic response to seeing her again stayed with me all the way home as I pondered on the ways of human nature. If that long forgotten tiny incident in my life evoked such resentful memories after so many years, what of the really important events and our feelings and emotions towards them? There was much food for thought here and my mind was beginning to open to such things.

Married life in Edinburgh suited me well but I did still have a cloud hanging over me. Frank was still working nights on the newspaper and when alone I could again sense spirit beings around me. I could not see them but I was very aware of their presence, even more so than before. I found it very stressful being alone in our lovely little house at night and this, along with a growing desire on my husband's part to change careers led to him finding another occupation. Now he, like most people, worked during the day and my nights were more peaceful. I could cope with strange "presences" with Frank by my side.

After a few years living in Corstorphine our son Scott was born. "Could life get any better?" I wondered. Well to be truthful, I suppose I would have preferred the house to ourselves, but as I was still only aware of "presences" and as I wasn't actually *seeing* anything or anybody, I managed to live with it. I still had no desire to understand more of what was going on around me, nor indeed would I have known where to start looking for help. Psychic "happenings" just weren't a subject for discussion amongst folk like us.

Soon, with some experience behind him in his new career Frank changed to a much better job and this meant a move to Forfar in Angus. As a family we settled in to life here very well. For both of us it was like coming home. Our daughter Alison (Ali) was born a few months later. Frank was very happy in his new job and life was good for me.

It seemed that the years of sensing spirit beings around me, and my nights of fear when I lived in Edinburgh, were over. I completely believe though that everything we experience in our lives, good or bad has a purpose. Sometimes it is the negative things that give us a push to change in some way and in retrospect we can then see that these are really blessings in disguise. In this case my growing inability to cope alone at night was the push Frank needed to change careers and this then led to our move to Forfar. Whether he would have made this change without any incentive I don't know, but I do know his career in paper sales was absolutely right for him. Who wouldn't like a job driving about with golf clubs in the boot of the car just in case a customer needed a partner for a game? This aspect of his work came under the heading of "building customer relationships". When he went on the various business golf outings (jollies to you and me) this was called "making new contacts". Yes Frank really enjoyed his new job, but the games of golf and the outings didn't happen all that often really, and in all fairness he worked very hard indeed the rest of the time and was very highly thought of by his company and his many business contacts.

Betty Fotheringham

CHAPTER 3

MY INTRODUCTION To

HEALING

This settled and happy life continued for some years and I really thought that all the spooky happenings were long gone, but sadly such was not the case. Some years on my nightly visitors found me again and there followed a period of what I still called "nightmares". But these were no nightmares in the real sense for I was always wide-awake. The difference now was that, as on that first night in Elgin so long before, I didn't only sense my visitors they were now clearly visible to me. Time after time I would wake up and there standing on one side of the bedroom or the other, would be perhaps one spirit being, sometimes two or three. As in my first encounter up in Elgin I would scream, but now Frank would hold and comfort me and my visitors would vanish.

I never told him the real cause of my distress. I preferred to keep up the pretence of nightmares. I had no explanation for what was happening to me and I

26

knew of no one who could help. This took a heavy toll on my nerves and Frank, with infinite patience and kindness, never once suggested that I needed a psychiatrist although this thought had passed through *my* mind a few times. Somehow I got through that part of my life telling no one of my problem but my fear of the supernatural steadily grew. For some considerable time, due to my spooky experiences, I had accepted that there was life after death. What kind of a life, I had no idea, and truthfully, I never felt any of these spirits to be unfriendly, watchful yes, but nothing more. On my part I was just totally at a loss to understand what was going on in my life and why me? Could it be that others had the same experiences and like me felt they could not discuss them? I did remember very clearly as a child, being told by my mother over and over again that I was "different". This went back to some of my first memories when I was only three. After I discovered around the age of thirteen that I had been adopted I assumed that this was what made me different. In the 1930's being illegitimate set you apart from others and your "history" went before you. This was very much so in the country and probably to a lesser extent in small towns where everyone knew all there was to know about you. Perhaps though there was another reason why I was different, and maybe my mother had sensed this around me.

Betty Fotheringham

I now know that some of us are born with a
close connection to the spirit world and for us seeing
spirit beings is relatively easy. For others, if they are
sufficiently interested, they can train themselves to be
clairvoyant. The word "clairvoyance" simply means
clear seeing or the ability to see into other worlds,
"clairaudience" means clear hearing, the ability to hear
from other worlds and "clairsentience" is clear sensing.
Usually we are better at one of these than the others
and I have not had any night-time visitors for many
years as I am now far more clairsentient than anything
else. We all have these extra senses buried somewhere
within us. Sometimes we recognise them at a time in
our lives when a loved one has passed on, and we feel
that person with us. What could be more natural than
that? But back at the time when all this was happening
to me, I believed it was all spooky and I wanted
nothing to do with it. Eventually though, help was at
hand, and it came to me through adversity. From a few
months after my marriage I suffered devastating
migraines and my life was getting to be very restricted.
Frank as always was my support, even though my
inability at times to do the things most young parents
did must have been frustrating for him.

One Saturday on a visit to our native Stonehaven
with our small caravan, I was struck down yet again
with a bad migraine, and our holiday weekend was
about to be ruined. A friend, on hearing of my plight,

suggested I see a local man, Bob Mitchell. She was sure he could help me. Now I had known Bob for years but I knew him to be an electrician. What could an electrician do for me, I wondered? On asking my friend she told me Bob was also a spiritual healer and was highly regarded as such in the area. Simultaneously, but quite separately, Frank had the same suggestion from another friend. Neither of us had heard of healing and I wasn't keen to find out more, but Frank insisted that I follow this advice. Even he felt that it was quite a coincidence for us both to be told of "healing" (whatever it was) for the first time in the space of one afternoon.

Within an hour of that visit I was 90% well. I experienced a miracle and Frank witnessed it. All Bob had done was ask me to sit on a chair while he placed his hands, first on my shoulders and then on my head. We stayed like that for less than ten minutes and this all took place in the back premises of his business. Bob wouldn't even accept any payment for his time. I visited him later at his home where he had a comfortable, friendly, specially built healing room with waiting room attached. Later I had longer appointments there and I knew my general health was improving with each visit. At the third visit Bob told me I too was a healer and in his opinion, in order to lead a fulfilled life, I should start channelling healing energy as he had done for years. This news was a bit of a shock to me and had I not been so badly in need of help I certainly would not have returned. More spooky stuff I thought.

However, on my return visits, and my health improved with each one, Bob, who is now a very dear friend by the way, quietly explained to me how healing "worked". I found it hard at first to understand his explanation of spiritual healing, yet he put it very simply. He believed there was an abundant healing energy available to us and on request this could be channelled through a healer to anyone who was in need of it. Well, far-fetched as that sounded to me, I could not deny the huge difference in my health as a direct result of my healing treatments through Bob.

Now between ghostly visits at night and healing hands by day, I was thoroughly confused. I admitted it was a lovely feeling sitting on a chair and letting this "energy" pour through my whole body and I so badly needed it, but "energy" was an unknown word to me in that context. I understood it to be something you had after a good night's sleep, and you used it up working all day. How could another person give you that? And where did it come from? God was the favoured source I was told, but God had been a complete stranger to me all my life. I even had to be christened a few days before my wedding. How embarrassing was that then – just because my natural mother and adoptive parents had never thought of it? On the croft God wasn't spoken about, except maybe contained in an expression of surprise, or if you hit your thumb with a hammer. After my marriage I did try church attendance for a little while, but I wasn't comfortable with the God portrayed there.

Now I was being asked by Bob, not only to believe this stuff, but to take part in it. He explained that all I had to do was relax, clear my mind of everyday trivia, tune in and ask to be used as a channel for the healing energy for whoever I was trying to help. Now I felt I could just about understand all that, except for the "tuning in" bit. What was that all about I wondered? It sounded a bit like turning on a radio and fiddling about until you found the right station. This was not too far from the truth as it turned out!

But I was having none of that I thought. This seemed a spooky world I would be getting myself into and I had no intention of going there. It entirely escaped me that with my sensing and seeing spirit people around me I had been living, albeit unwillingly, in this spooky world for years. But we see only what we want to see.

Then a friend who was quite unwell and who had witnessed what healing had done for me, asked if I would take her to see Bob. This I readily did and he immediately seized this opportunity to get me to place my hands on my friend's shoulders while he

31

placed his hands near, but not touching mine. (I only agreed to this to save embarrassment and perhaps to prove that Bob was wrong in his assertion that I was a healer.) However I can only describe the sensation I had as like being transported to another world. A feeling of deep peace surrounded me and I felt a surge of energy pass through my hands into my friend's body. *Now* I understood the "energy" thing and to some extent the "tuning in" bit. After a few minutes I found the courage to open my eyes and there was Bob sitting down in the far corner of the room. *I* was the channel for this wonderful energy and I could hardly believe it for it had all happened in an instant. I now know that we all, without exception, have healing ability. Some have to develop it and others, as was the case with me, can manifest it instantly. Healing is probably the most natural, gentle, non-invasive therapy there is. Although we all have the ability to be a healer, sadly not everyone is suited to it. Those first few minutes when I was aware of the healing energy pouring through me to my friend, changed my life forever. Bob talked quite openly about his "helpers" from the spirit world and how we all had them guiding and supporting us. He explained they could only help if we asked them to do so, for we all have freewill and they must wait for an invitation from us. This aspect of healing started to intrigue me. Could my helpers actually be that bunch in my bedroom every night? I didn't think so. I wasn't buying into that.

This very limited experience of healing though, made me look again at how I viewed God. If this wonderful feeling I got when healing did indeed come from God, then this was a God I could accept unreservedly. I suppose I could say I had found spirituality and lost religion.

I would like to make it clear before I go any further that channelling healing does not necessarily require a connection through a guide. Many healers in the past worked this way, but the healing energy is available directly providing we are on the right wavelength. I do believe though that my initial connection to it through a guide was right for me at that time. Later, with more experience, I was able to find the right wavelength on my own, and when I came to teach healing this was our method of training. (Our organisation was non-denominational, as of course is healing.) For those who are interested, just a brief word about wavelengths, (if you wish just skip this bit). Our brain has four rhythms or rates of vibration. For everyday activities it ticks over at the Beta level, 14-28 cycles per second. When we meditate or sometimes even in a daydream, it slips into Alpha at 7-14 cps. In deep meditation it moves to Theta, 4-7cps. There is a fourth level, which is Delta, but here we are in an almost trancelike or unconscious state. Changing the brainwave to access the healing energy flow was what Bob called "tuning in". It was some time though before I understood all this. It was sufficient for me at first to just "feel" or "sense" when I was tuned in. I would experience a feeling of deep peace. I was beginning to feel that in my life I was piecing together a huge jigsaw and that I was getting one little piece at a time. I decided that this suited me just fine. I could only cope with a little at a time because my understanding of the world I lived in was being turned on its head.

Meantime, on a Saturday again, a church notice in our local paper caught my eye. I'm sure I'd never even glanced at these church notices before that time, but the word "healing" just jumped out at me. Didn't I say we see what we want to see? This was a spiritualist church advertising their services and healing evenings. This church was in Dundee and this was a lot nearer than Stonehaven for me. Just maybe I could go to this church and get the benefits of healing, but not be persuaded to do any.

Attending one of the other services prior to risking the healing evenings appealed to me, as I knew nothing of mediumship but I was now very curious. Perhaps I should explain here that a spiritualist medium's aim is to prove life after death, usually by giving "messages" from departed relatives or friends. If these messages should contain information only available to the people concerned, this is usually accepted as proof of life after death. I know you will probably be thinking that these things can be hoaxed, and we have all seen that explained on television many times, but I quickly learned to sort the wheat from the chaff when it came to mediums. Another learning experience.

I went along to that first Wednesday afternoon meeting with a friend, and we stood outside on the other side of the street for a very long time before entering this, to me anyway, scary place. That afternoon I did get a "message" which I considered proved absolutely nothing at all. I was prejudiced of course, particularly since it echoed Bob's advice to become a healer and I didn't want to know that. Not only do we see what we want to see, we hear only what we want to hear.

My curiosity had been aroused though because, as I had found with our landlady and her daughter in Edinburgh, the people I met at the Church of the Spirit were very normal, kind and welcoming. They weren't at all pushy with their beliefs and indeed I was told to accept nothing that was said unless I was comfortable with it. This was continually repeated to me.

The next night I went for healing. That again was a wonderful experience. There were four healers and we had the choice of sitting on one of the chairs and having healing, or we could just sit at the back of the church and enjoy the peaceful atmosphere. Following this we went through to another room, sat round a table and had a cup of tea. How much more down to earth could that have been? The healers and helpers in the kitchen were also kind, sincere people giving up their time for no reward whatsoever, and some of them had been doing this for years.

The benefit I received from healing, first with Bob and then in the church, was immense for before this I had been on antibiotics for repeated infections and painkillers and tranquilisers for migraines. I felt I had a reserved seat in the doctor's waiting room for what were almost weekly visits. In other words I was a complete mess and felt I was on a treadmill of illness from which I could see no escape.

Perhaps I should mention here that spiritualism is a recognised religion and it served me well at a time in my life when I needed to find God. In recent years I have had no connection to any church but I live with the knowledge that God isn't only found in a specified building on a certain day. He is with me 24/7. I have long chats with him, somewhat one-sided I admit. (This is usually called praying!) I hasten to say here before I offend anyone that I am not knocking churches, it is just that they don't seem right for me at this time. Who knows though what the future may hold? After all with all my initial scepticism who would have thought I would spend well over thirty years being a healer – and teaching it at that? I'm sure God is laughing in the background as I write this. Some wise soul once said, "If you want to make God laugh, tell him your plans." I told him a while ago that I didn't want to write another book, especially one on healing, and here I am. Over many years my perception of God has changed considerably and I may share this with you later. What I can say now is that when I accepted the concept of healing and my part in it, I found the reason for my life and I wouldn't change one minute of that for anything.

CHAPTER 4

PROOF OF SPIRIT

(nothing to do with whisky!)

This scary world and place that I had fallen into reminded me a little of Alice in Wonderland but it started to feel very friendly indeed, and I joined the Church of the Spirit for a few years. Soon I had many very good friends there. Of course too it would be good to say that my own health was made perfect and I lived happily ever after. What I can say is that my experiences there opened my eyes to the fact that there are many ways of healing, many alternatives to allopathic medicine, and what suits one person may not suit another. My horizons were widening all the time and quite a few pieces of my jigsaw fell effortlessly into place.

I was now meeting people who had tried different alternative therapies, and I was fascinated by some of them. Although my own health vastly improved I still had a little way to go, and I was now greedy for still more improvement and also for a greater knowledge of esoteric things and other ways of healing.

While living in Edinburgh I had been personal assistant (a fancy name for a secretary by the way) to a peer of the realm and before that, secretary to two solicitors, but I had never felt comfortable with my career. I just didn't fit in or I felt this to be so. (This was partly due no doubt to my shorthand skills being a bit dicey.) I must add too that this career was chosen for me by the headmaster of my primary school. My dream of becoming an assistant in a chemist's shop fell on deaf ears. This totally unsuitable career ended of course when my first pregnancy reached three months. I had to leave my job. This was normal at the time. It wouldn't have done to have a visibly pregnant member of staff in any professional office. Women were encouraged to hide their pregnant state as soon as possible, usually by wearing very baggy clothes to hide the bump!

But now here was another avenue opening up for me. Amongst other healers and spiritually aware people, for the first time in my life *I didn't feel different.* Can you try to imagine how that felt? At last I had come home as it were. I must have been a real pain to the people in the Church of the Spirit at that time for I wanted to learn and experience everything.

As a result of the influence of Bob and my new friends in the spiritualist church I did finally start seriously practising healing, tentatively at first, but soon with growing confidence. This was getting to be not such a strange business after all. I didn't discuss it much though outside the church. I wasn't yet ready for questions. This was just as well for by the time I did "go public" I was strong enough to ignore the ridicule and the persuasion to see the error of my ways.

I often enjoy walking down by Forfar Loch near where I live and some time ago a circle of ground was set aside, a low wall was built around this circle and spring bulbs were planted through the grass. There is also a small tree there. A stone was erected with simple wording – "The Forfar Witches. Just People". I have a great affinity with this small area of ground and pause often to think that if I had been born some years earlier the words on this stone would have applied to me. A sobering thought indeed. I now feel proud that I did eventually find the courage to hold my head high during those early years and state "I am a spiritual healer". I am also just a person.

Back to the story. There were no training courses in healing available in Scotland then. They came later and I was proud to be part of the teaching team within the main healing organisation in the country at that time. There was training in mediumship available within the spiritualist church and this was my next step. At this

40

time healing, mediumship and spiritualism were almost always connected, or perceived to be so. Probably this was because most healers were mediumistic or believed to be. There was some healing taking place within other churches and indeed for a time I was involved in healing discussions within the Church of Scotland of which at that time I was still a member. This of course was never referred to as "spiritual" healing and I was told at the time by the minister that only ordained ministers could "lay hands" on others. I was also firmly told that I would only be allowed to "discuss" healing within the church. Incidentally the word spiritual when used in the context of healing simply means healing mind, body and *spirit*. It has no connection to spiritualism, although as I have already said, many spiritualists are healers. I have also already said we are all healers, and we all have the ability to link in to a higher vibrational level, it is just that we either have no desire to or have not yet learned how to. Now most healers refer to themselves as energy healers, some are Reiki healers and there are many others. The healing energy all comes from the same source which at the moment I will call God but I will explain what I mean by that later. Please bear with me I've so much to say and I can't get it all down fast enough!

From having little interest in religion I now had a foot in two camps. One of the major differences between the two that I found was that, in the Church of Scotland I was *told* what to believe, but in the Church of the Spirit I was repeatedly told to accept only what felt right for me. I preferred the latter approach and the perception of God I came to know there was right for me at that time.

Once I had made up my mind to risk mediumship development (an enormous leap for me at the time), I was lucky enough to get a place in a development group, and so I started my education with the hope that I wasn't going to have to be clever to develop as a medium. I don't do clever. As it turned out it didn't matter much as my development within that group was short lived. At the meetings we would sit in a room with only a red light to see by and after an opening prayer by the leader, we relaxed and asked if anyone wanted to "come through". Now this seemed a bit too like the "Is there anybody there?" jokes from television for my comfort. However in spite of this attitude it didn't take me long to make my first spirit contact. Maybe some of my night-time visitors were just waiting their chance to get their word in. This communicator of mine had been a schoolteacher when alive and a real bossy boots she must have been. For those of you who may be interested, the physical sensation I had was of my body filling out (I was reasonably slim at that time) and I felt myself growing taller. Mentally I felt quite superior and haughty. I was decidedly uncomfortable with this. I found myself pointing and shaking a finger at my fellow sitters as I passed on her message. It was of such great import that I have no idea now what it was. The changes I felt in my physical body I was told were due to me sensing the body of this schoolteacher contact when she lived on earth. Was this it? Was this what it was all about? Surely there had to be more to it than this. I don't really know what I expected. In my ignorance perhaps I thought I would be having a long chat with some very wise being, but maybe they were all busy somewhere else that night. However I soon learned more about spirit contacts. It seemed that as a complete novice I was only able to make contact with the first level in the spirit world. Obviously this was where bossy schoolteachers hung out! With more experience I quickly learned to reach higher levels as this was essential in order for me to be a good healing channel. Meantime back to the church library to study more and I decided to give development groups a miss for a time. Bossy schoolteachers didn't hold any appeal for me.

It would be easy to say that all the sensations I felt that night were the result of an overactive imagination. Indeed at the time this would have been my preferred explanation. But it wasn't as cut and dried as that, and remember too, my friends in the church kept telling me to reject anything I wasn't comfortable with. This I tried to do until a most extraordinary thing happened.

One week the church was having an evening of what was called "Transfiguration" by a lady called Queenie Nixon. I was eager to go to prove to myself as much as anything, that it was all a load of rubbish, and so I was in a 100% negative frame of mind about what I was about to witness. I left later that evening with my mind in a state of total confusion. Queenie was very small in stature and her "guide" was said to be very tall and of North American Indian origin. Aye, I thought, how many times have I heard that? There seemed to be a lot of N.A. Indian guides about. How could I know at that time that I would in later years visit America and spend time with some wonderful Indian people who were very spiritual. Where was my scepticism then?

Back to the church where we were told that this guide would be the intermediary between the spirit beings or "contacts" and the medium. The lights were switched off, leaving one small red light shining upwards on to the medium's face. She was wearing a black garment and really all we could see was her face and head. "Very theatrical" I thought.

We were told that in a demonstration of "Transfiguration", when a medium made a contact through a guide, the medium's features would change to resemble those of the contact. A member of the audience would hopefully recognise the features as those of a deceased family member or friend and the message would be for that person. I didn't get a message and nor did I want one. I wanted to concentrate hard on this phenomenon in order to understand it. Although I had a huge thirst for knowledge I wasn't going to be taken in.

Well, messages came and were gratefully accepted, sometimes with tears. Now and again I thought I saw the medium's features change, but overall I was seriously disappointed. Then something happened that shook me to the core. Queenie announced that before we all left, her guide, the North American Indian fellow had a message for us. As clearly as can be I saw Queenie's head and top part of her body change. The face I saw was well over a foot above the height of the medium's head that I had been closely watching all evening. The features were fairly typical of a North American Indian and the headdress above that was magnificent. Could I have imagined all that? I knew I hadn't. There were gasps from all around me so I knew I wasn't alone in seeing what was before me.

I have no recollection of the message, if I ever heard it. I was so astounded by what I could clearly see. Soon, with the message delivered, everyone filed out of the room and I rushed to the front and checked the space behind the rostrum. I was looking for a stool or anything the medium could have stood on to give her the extra height that I had so clearly noted. There was absolutely nothing there. I realise of course that this still could not have explained the change of facial features

45

and the headdress. That evening gave me a lot to think about for a very long time to come. My scepticism was dwindling. Now I have no trouble accepting what I saw although I am a long way from explaining it. However *Spiritual Alchemy* written by Dr Christine Page does it beautifully.

Around that same time the church organised an evening of clairvoyance by an international medium called Gordon Higginson who came from London. Being so new to spiritualism his reputation was unknown to me but I knew he was regarded by others as a highly respected medium. This event was held in the Marryat Hall in Dundee and on the night in question this was almost full.

I repeat, before this visit I hadn't met this man and that evening I sat in the middle of the audience staying out of sight as much as possible, and away from other church members. I was very much in my "I'll believe it if I see it" frame of mind again. At one point the medium said he had a message for a healer from a place called "For...far". He pronounced Forfar as two words. I sat very still for, although curious, would never have publicly claimed to be a healer. Getting no response the medium then said "I will spell the surname of this person, it is "Forthingham". I was rather shaken by this because although not the correct spelling of my surname, it was very near it. I was pushed by friends some distance away to own up. The message was said to be from my brother Wullie who had died of cancer not that long before this time. Again I was being urged by him now to seriously do more healing. Other personal stuff was mentioned too, including the fact that in a certain bookcase in my home I had a photograph of two well-known healers of that time. This was said to be next to a little book of prayer with a blue cover. I knew I had such a book but I was definite that I had no photos of any healers in that bookcase or in any other place in my home. At that time I was still keeping a tight lid on this newly found interest of mine.

My brother also mentioned meeting again his first child, Gladys, who had died in infancy. This was quite a shock to me too for only very close family would know of this baby and even some of my brothers were unaware that this little soul had been christened Gladys only hours before she died. I was only four at the time. This reminded me too that in a conversation with my sister in law Violet, she had confided in me that, in the hours leading up to Wullie's death, he had spoken a few times about the beautiful teenage girl he saw standing by his bed. Although he could clearly see her he was unaware of her identity. At the time I sensed that this was little Gladys. I went home from that meeting that evening with very mixed feelings. I was, as said before, totally convinced about life after death. This had been reinforced through my involvement with the spiritualist church. I had never had this certainty in all the years I had been a member of the Church of Scotland. I didn't disbelieve what I was told there, but I preferred to keep an open mind. Now I was more than certain and I was now having to, so reluctantly, accept that communication between the two worlds was also possible. I had come a very long way since my first scary ghostly visit up in Elgin when I still lived on the croft, and that evening I found a few more pieces that fitted perfectly into my jigsaw.

Halfway home to Forfar that night I suddenly saw in my mind my annual Christmas card envelope from Wullie and his wife Violet. The spelling of my surname on that envelope was the same as given in the message. It was very late that night when I phoned Violet and asked her to spell my name. She wasn't too pleased for she had been in bed, but she spelt it just the same. Her spelling of my surname matched that of the message. Violet and I shed a few tears while on the phone that night when I told her my tale, and then she shared a secret with me. I had been so hesitant about telling her of my experience for after all my brother, her husband, had only recently died and she was still grieving. Was my tale going to comfort her by proving that Wullie lived on, or was it going to upset her even more? I needn't have worried, she told me that her sister, who now lived in Australia was a medium. Now that was news to me, but it helped me share other things freely with Violet as time went on. I now accepted beyond any doubt that this message had indeed come from my brother.

Still, I checked the bookcase mentioned to prove that at least this part of the message was wrong. I quickly found the little blue covered book and there, next to it, was a photograph of Ray and Joan Branch of the Harry Edwards Healing Sanctuary in Surrey. This photo was on a book cover and that possibility had never occurred to me.

Before I move on from "messages," just a couple more. Some time before this, within my family, a young man had been killed when his motorcycle had left the road in completely inexplicable circumstances. The message this time was said to be from this young man and again it came through another international medium, who told me that this relative often spent time in my home, and I would have seen him as a bright spot of light in a certain corner of our sitting room. This indeed was true for this light had often intrigued me, but I had always dismissed it as my eyes playing tricks. Through the medium this young man told me the full story of his bike crash and the reason for it. He had died instantly at the scene of the accident and no medium could have had this information. This young man was the grandson of my brother Wullie. Another famous medium of the time was Albert Best. He was Irish and had a strong accent. Because of this he was a little difficult to understand as he also spoke very quickly. Albert was a good friend of Louise Hill, who was the President of the Church of the Spirit at that time, and he visited the church in Dundee frequently. On this occasion I was lucky enough to get a private sitting with him. At that time private sittings cost very little and most mediums, even the well-known ones, made only a modest living. I was excited at the prospect of my first private sitting with a well-known medium for I had no idea what this involved, and I remember also feeling very brave although nervous. At the time it seemed a very daring thing to do as I was still keeping this side of my life very quiet even from my friends. I was leading a double life and I was dreading the possibility of anyone from Forfar visiting the church and recognising me. It never occurred to me that if this happened they too might not wish to be recognised. This of course did eventually happen and the world did not come to an end as a result of it.

Before this appointment I meditated, (fancy me a country quine meditating!) and asked if the medium could give me any information regarding my healing. I knew my friend Bob had a healing guide and I had been told that I too had one, but did I really believe this? Up to that point I had never had any awareness of any spirit being around me while I was healing. Remember my experience of spirits had not been happy occasions up until then so if I did have a guide, I definitely wanted to know a bit about him or her, and I certainly didn't want it to be the bossy schoolteacher. When the exciting day of my sitting came, Albert gave me all the answers to the questions I had asked in my meditation. My guide was said to have been a German doctor who had specialised in back problems. This sounded better than my bossy schoolteacher. I asked for a name and was told I could call him Dr. Hans, although this was not his name when alive. Apparently the spirit world didn't go in for names much. That always seemed a pity to me for we set great store by them down here. I was given details of his medical qualifications and where he lived when he was last on earth. Of course I was now getting more and more interested and intrigued by all this. I was particularly impressed with the fact that I had actually got answers to the questions I had privately asked a few days before the meeting. Absolutely no one knew I had done this.

Although proof was now coming to me thick and fast I still wanted more. I set one more test. This time the medium was a lady I had known for some time and before going to that service I meditated again and asked for more proof. Again I got a message about the part I needed to play in healing. I asked the medium for the name of my healing guide. She said that it was a man and he was looking very cross, he wouldn't give a name but kept waving his hands in front of her face. I said "His name is Dr. Hans". Now at last I was prepared to believe. To believe that when circumstances are right we can indeed communicate with other worlds. But even more important to me was the belief that I could help others by channelling healing when requested to do so. I was now totally committed.

After spending some time in another mediumship group within the church where I was extremely comfortable, made some very good friends and really did learn a great deal, I was asked to join the group of church healers and I was very proud of this privilege. I was now totally in my comfort zone and I still completely believe that it is a great privilege to be given the opportunity to help anyone in this way. According to the leader of the church healing group I was considered to be a very old soul indeed. I hadn't a clue what that meant for I hadn't at that time made any study of reincarnation. That, and the experiences connected with this fascinating subject were still to come.

Because I was now seeing members of the public and even though I was making no charge or even accepting donations, I decided that I needed some accreditation. With the help of my good friend Bob and that of George, who was the leader of the church healing group at that time, I was able to get membership of the national healing organisation I referred to earlier. This was the organisation that I eventually tutored with for about ten years. Being a member of this organisation also gave me insurance cover for working with members of the public. This was not all that important at that time but is essential today.

CHAPTER 5

REINCARNATION OR DYING TO LIVE?

As I said earlier on one of my first visits to the Church of the Spirit, George, who led the healing team, commented that I was a "very old soul indeed". At the time this meant nothing to me but my curiosity was aroused and my mind started to connect that remark with the odd bits of conversation I overheard about reincarnation.

Well it was back to the church library again and more reading. I had been making full use of this facility at the church since I joined. I can devour a book in a day and then spend the evening feeling guilty about my laziness. My upbringing didn't include books you see. Indeed my mother considered that women had no need of them. There were no libraries in schools and town libraries excluded those who did not have a town address. I've been making up for all those lost years ever since.

So I read everything I could on reincarnation. It must have been about this time too that I found the Mind, Body and Spirit shelves in Waterstone's bookshop in Dundee. What joy and excitement! With access to all these books and so many new fascinating subjects to study, I thought I had died and gone to heaven. Well not quite, I'm exaggerating a little here, a bad habit of mine.

However, as with the other stuff, reincarnation slowly started to make perfect sense to me. I had at times pondered on this Heaven we are told about. In my case this was at school because the busy life at home on the croft didn't leave much time for discussions on Heaven, but when I was at school religious education was still being taught there. In my ignorance I had wondered how there was room for everyone up there, so a bit of recycling seemed like a good idea to me. Then I thought about that feeling of familiarity we sometimes get in a place that we know we have never been to before. Reincarnation would seem to give us an answer to this too. By the way I am aware that there are other very valid explanations for these feelings.

Now I was still following the advice I had been given when starting on this journey of exploration and that was to only believe what felt right to me. To help me in this I read, along with many others, a few books about children who had been born with clear memories of past lives. The cases I read of had been very well researched and were found to be completely genuine. To me too they sounded totally convincing. I now believe that we are all spiritual beings having an earthly life. When the time is right we cast off our physical body (die in other words) and return home. Then, again when the time is right, we may choose to return to another life on earth. I do sometimes think we must be mad – as if one life on this earth wasn't enough. To keep repeating this seems to me a bit masochistic. But we do all this in order to learn and develop. What are we supposed to be learning? To put it as simply as I can we are learning to live this and all our lives for the good of the whole and not for our own ends. This has to include taking care of our planet and indeed we must be mindful always of the effect of our actions on the whole of the universe. In the next chapter I will explain my understanding of this to the best of my ability, but it has taken me many years to reach this point. I like to think now that I tread lightly upon this earth for there is no doubt she can manage very well without me but I cannot survive in this human body without her.

Again to help me accept the possibility that we all live many lives another few spooky experiences came my way. So what's new about that? The first one was powerful but gentle. Frank and I were visiting a nearby castle for me to explore the gardens. Frank didn't enjoy these jaunts much. He could just be persuaded to wander round the outside of an old house or castle as long as I didn't suggest going inside. "I'm not paying to go in there!" he would say. With my love of gardens I was mostly happy with that. Isn't any good marriage built on compromise? After all I love our Scottish mountains, but I prefer to love them from a comfy four wheeled vehicle. I also love sitting by beautiful lochs but I have no desire to fish them. Two of Frank's hobbies were hill walking and fishing and I was never tempted, even a little, to share them. I did not therefore expect him to wander round inside old buildings with *me*.

For me just seeing a castle in the distance brought a feeling of excitement, although I have never had any desire to live in one. On the occasion that I mention, we were wandering around in the grounds of this castle and my eyes were drawn to a smallish window at the rear of the building some way up from the ground. Suddenly, quite clearly in my mind, I saw myself as little more than a child working in this castle as a scullery maid. The window I was looking at was on the servants' stair and I saw myself sitting in it for a few moments at a time to catch a glimpse of the outside world. I "knew" this building had been my home for a time and perhaps buried unhappy memories of this past lifetime is why I have no great desire to live in a castle this time round, although they do interest me.

I am aware that for many of you this experience could be explained differently, as could the others I will relate to you. But there will be many more of you who will understand my conviction because you too will have had similar moments of just "knowing" things. We should pay great heed to these moments by the way. We could learn a lot by doing so. Sadly we usually dismiss them as "fanciful" or "all in our head".

Some time later Frank and I spent holidays in France and there I had another two experiences. They were totally different, but each in its own way hugely added to my spiritual understanding. First I have to admit that I have never been one for travelling. I went to France to please Frank. France was near enough to drive to. In my eyes that was all it had going for it. I wouldn't have to get on a plane. At that time my ears didn't do planes. That came later.

I hated most of that first holiday and our rented apartment was such a disaster that we moved into a hotel in the middle of the two weeks for a break. That was my first holiday abroad and it wasn't a great start.

As we were self-catering, we set off the day after our arrival to find a supermarket. For some reason we missed the town we were heading for and found ourselves in Rheims at a roundabout with about a hundred streets off it. (I'm exaggerating again.) This was our first big city roundabout driving on the "wrong" side of the street and Frank needed a few minutes to get his bearings. He decided to take the first street off and this led us to a quiet little car park with empty spaces where we parked, ate our picnic lunch and then went exploring on foot. So we were in that area of Rheims by sheer chance.

We strolled along a street chosen at random, rounded a corner and there before us was Rheims Cathedral. We were approaching it from the back but I immediately knew this was *my* building. Tears welled up and I felt physically sick with excitement. I wanted to stay in that spot and look at it forever, but at the same time I couldn't wait to get round to the front and inside. I also had this strange feeling that I wanted to kneel. Thank goodness I resisted that impulse, as my long-suffering husband might just have left me there.

On entering the cathedral through magnificent doors I couldn't control my emotions. Leaving Frank I ran from pillar to pillar, I wasn't exploring, I was remembering. I knew I had been a nun, I had lived nearby and this was my place of worship. I had come home. When Frank caught up with me I asked if I might spend a little time on my own in prayer. There were quiet areas for this purpose. Frank readily agreed as he could see how very deeply affected I was, although he would never guess the reason. It would be a little time before I could discuss reincarnation with him, if ever.

I had left behind in Scotland three special people who were diagnosed as terminally ill, and I wanted to send healing energy to them from this wonderful building. (I describe my introduction to this in Chapter 7.) I sat down, relaxed and tuned in. I felt as if the top of my head opened and I was in contact directly with God. Words were unnecessary – He knew my thoughts. I have never experienced anything quite like that since but feel so privileged to have done so even once. Those moments spent in that cathedral will live with me forever.

The next story has nothing to do with reincarnation but as it happened in France on that same holiday it seems a good time to relate it. It has though got a lot to do with how sensitive healers are or can become. On our last full day of that French holiday and this was *so* out of character, Frank suggested we visit a nearby cathedral that had been bomb damaged during the Second World War and was only now being repaired. This building, although very beautiful, had stood largely unused in the intervening years. This was something we found very strange on that first visit to France. We imagined that after the German occupation was over all bad memories of that time would have been removed. But this was not so as everywhere we went we found reminders of that time. Our flat, which was attached to the mayor's office, had German helmets, bits of uniform and other leftovers from the occupation all in full view. This contributed greatly to our dislike of living there. Frank had been in Belgium, France and Germany just at the end of the war. One of my brothers had been seriously injured at the start of this war and that affected his whole life. Again at the start of the war another brother Alfie was at Dunkirk and he was said to be the last airman to escape from there in a tiny fishing boat when the Germans overran the area. Our memories of the Second World War were not good and we didn't appreciate reminders of it on a holiday so many years on.

We entered the main part of this cathedral (the damage was all to the rear of the building) and after a few minutes of wandering round I started to feel faint and quite ill. I made an excuse and went outside for a little to recover. Back at our car I was absolutely fine. Twice more I went back into that building and each time had to leave to prevent fainting. I sat in the car deeply upset at my behaviour. After all Frank rarely entered buildings except to please me and here I was wimping out.

When he joined me a little later he gave me a possible explanation for my very physical symptoms. Inside to the rear of this church he had found a large plaque erected some time after the war. It told a sombre tale. Some of the villagers had been suspected of harbouring and supporting members of the French resistance. The occupying German soldiers used the church to torture the suspects. When this didn't bring the confessions they wanted, one villager was shot each day, including their priest. Can you imagine the buildup

of terror in that building? Frank explained that he was
sure that this atmosphere, even after many years, was
the reason for my physical symptoms. He had felt the
negativity in this building too, but to a much lesser
extent. On reading its history he knew the cause. This
incident was a huge lesson to me on protecting myself
from negativity at all times and I was becoming more
aware that my sensitivity to my surroundings and
particularly atmospheres, was growing as my healing
abilities developed. On a lighter note we returned to
France a couple of years later, stayed in another part of
the country and had a wonderful holiday.

Over the years since my experience in Rheims
Cathedral, I have been aware of other places I felt were
very familiar to me. Possibly I had been to some of
them in a past life, but as I said earlier, I am also aware
that there are other explanations for these feelings,
probably easier to believe. It is so important to question
everything and only accept what we feel comfortable
with. I am now very comfortable with the belief that I
have lived many lives.

CHAPTER 6

ENERGY? WHAT IS THIS ENERGY?

Because I keep referring to energy I feel I need to give as coherent an explanation as possible, of how I view this energy and its source. Please don't skip this bit. It is important and to some extent it explains my view of the God thing. I suppose my understanding, still incomplete by a long way I'm sure, of just what healing energy is, where it comes from and how it works, even at a distance, became much clearer when I started to read up on quantum physics. I have to admit I was mighty lost at times, drowning in a sea of words that I didn't understand, and some of them of such recent origin that my dictionary couldn't help, but eventually it did begin to sink in and I intend to keep at it. The purchase of an up to date dictionary wouldn't go amiss either.

I now know that the universe and our earth is part of it, is one vast moving field of energy. (We are continually being told this, but I don't think we realise the full implications of it.) Every single thing in our world is energy vibrating at different rates. Now that means human beings, the rocks and mountains in our landscape, the planets, our trees and plants and oh just everything you can think of, and all that we don't even see or know about. The rate of vibration governs whether we can actually see anything or not. When I was teaching I liked to explain this by using the example of the spokes on a bicycle wheel. Now, when stationary or moving very slowly, all the spokes are clearly visible. As the cycle speeds up the spokes disappear. This just means they are moving too fast for us to see – *but they are still there*. Now that's the bit we need to pay attention to. We too readily dismiss things because they don't fit our individual belief system. This was my huge problem when I started to see spirit people on a regular basis. It would have been such a relief for me to share my fears but no-one in my circle would have believed me, except perhaps my mother, because she too had seen a "ghost" when a teenager. Spirit people vibrate at a different rate to that of us, and that is the only reason most people cannot see them.

We are happy to plug into another energy that we cannot see – i.e. electricity. Do we deny *its* existence? No, and we would be lost without it. So how about opening our minds to other unseen energies? This universal energy is often referred to as "the field", sometimes as "the source" and, wait for it – "the God energy". Some years ago I learned a great deal from a book called *The Field* written by Lynne McTaggart. This book confirmed so much of what I already knew, but in places the information contained there stretched my mind even further. I suppose it shouldn't have done, for had I not already had many spooky or unexplained things happening to me? Incidentally I do consider that my upbringing in the country, living so close to nature, has been a huge advantage to me. I feel I developed a natural sensitivity to things unseen. That doesn't mean they didn't scare me at times, but it isn't so surprising that when I did open my mind to such things, I learned quite fast. And I was able to keep a level head and sort the possible from the downright silly. Of course to quote Stephen Hawking "What now appears as the paradoxes of quantum theory will seem just common sense to our children's children." At one time remember, man believed our earth to be flat.

For a number of years too, a friend and I went to London to attend weekend conferences organised by Lynne McTaggart, to hear lectures by some of the leading people in the field of quantum physics and other subjects. These speakers were from many different parts of the world. My friend and I would leave Edinburgh airport very early in the morning on the Saturday and on arrival, we would find our way into London and be waiting for the doors of the venue to open for a 9.30a.m. start, having snatched some breakfast somewhere along the way. We were glued to our seats, sometimes I admit, nodding off from sheer exhaustion due to lack of sleep and excitement. We shared a room on most of these trips and tired though we were, after going to bed we would talk until the first signs of daylight started to creep in to the sky. Arriving back home it would take a week for my system to return to normal, but oh the excitement of those trips and the mind blowing lectures. One in particular was by Edgar Mitchell, the sixth American astronaut to land on the moon. I missed my lunch that day as he was generous enough to give a few of us his time in a corner of the hall after his lecture had finished. To meet and talk with an astronaut even for only a few minutes was for me, a dizzy height indeed. It was this astronaut who commented that "There are no unnatural or supernatural phenomena, only very large gaps in our knowledge."

So this boundless energy is all around us, and remember too, our bodies are part of this energy. I read somewhere that quantum physics defines this energy field as "invisible moving forces that influence the physical realm". We inhabit this physical realm because of our particular rate of vibration. There are other realms or levels as I prefer to call them, possibly many, all vibrating at a different rate to ours, probably all inhabited and I believe we can access at least some of these other vibrational levels if we learn how to do so. If you are finding all this talk of invisibility a little hard to believe, think back to my mention earlier of electricity, (never mind all the other invisibles such as radio waves etc.,) without a plug and switch on electricity remains invisible and it is only when we decide to access it that we see it in the shape of warmth from a fire or boiling water from a kettle.

Now I see this connection to all things and all people a bit like a giant web. Our slightest movement registers around the universe, and more surprising even than that, our very thoughts affect those around us and at any distance! In one way this is scary, but in another way it is extremely comforting. Knowing and accepting this encourages us to dump the negative stuff we hang on to, and fill our minds with kind positive thoughts about others and ourselves. And if you think this is easy, think again, I have been trying to perfect this for years and I don't always win. That I suppose is because I'm human and if I were perfect then I would possibly shift in to the next level and start again. (This is usually referred to as dying, by the way.) If you find this connection to the thoughts of others a bit hard to accept, again stop and consider, how often have you known who was on the telephone before you picked it up? How often have you decided to phone someone only to have them phone you first? How often have you said "I just knew that was what you were going to say"? See what I mean? We just can't ignore it, can we? And coincidence can't explain it all.

Let's go back to the astronaut Ed Mitchell for just a minute. At the conference in London he shared with us what was a life changing experience for him. He said that after completing their information gathering on the moon and when their spaceship was heading back to earth, he was suddenly overwhelmed by a strange but wonderful feeling of connectedness, and he even spoke of this web of energy that seemed to connect the whole of the universe, all people, their thoughts and feelings. Doesn't that just echo all that I have been telling you? Unfortunately I didn't take many notes at the lectures but most of this you can read up on in the book I mentioned by Lynne called *The Field*.

Making contact with this field is exactly how healers can channel energy to those who request it. This is the "tuning in" bit that I had the problem with at the start of my healing career. And this takes me right back to my explanation of wavelengths. To access this field we have to be on the right wavelength. How do we do that, I hear you ask?

Well I was very lucky in that I seemed to have a natural ability for this. However this ability only got me to the next level and I did say earlier that at the beginning of my healing, I channelled energy to people assisted by a healing guide, Dr Hans. I was strongly advised at that time to learn to meditate. This was sound advice and as I became more and more proficient in this practice, I felt the presence of Dr

Hans less and less. This was simply because I was now able to reach a higher energy level on my own. Meditation, and more on this later, is a very valuable tool for all of us to master at this time in our history. It would be to the benefit of all if guidance on this was freely available on the NHS. Hopefully it is.

Before I move on to something else I will tell you a little more about this energy and our physical bodies. We all have an energy field around our body. Indeed I repeat all matter has an energy field. My first intro to seeing these energy fields was by looking at trees. I found that I needed to relax my body and particularly my gaze, and let go of all preconceived ideas on this subject. If I then chose a tree with the sky as a background, and preferably on a bright day but not looking directly into the sun, and if I looked at the centre of the tree, I would see with my peripheral vision a blue/violet/grey shadow around the outer edge of the tree. I then graduated to the pot plants on my window ledge and realised that I had been seeing their energy field for a very long time without knowing what it was and even more astonishing, I had never questioned it.

After some practice I moved on to looking at my hands against a white background and there it was again. Not so difficult after all. Later again when I was teaching all this stuff I would demonstrate and encourage my students to experiment with measuring this energy field with dowsing rods or a pendulum.

(Again, more on that later.) The "graveyard" slot (just after lunch) was the perfect time for this – it kept everyone awake and interested, including me. Yes, tutors get drowsy after lunch too.

This energy field around the body is what we call the aura. Sadly this word is often misused, but you at least will now know the true meaning of it. It extends a little way out from the body and how far depends upon our health, mood, spiritual awareness and so on. The stronger our energy fields are, the better protected we are from negativity. Quite a few years ago now a camera was developed that could photograph this energy field around our bodies. Yes, seriously – *proof* – the invisible made visible! Some therapists can even diagnose health problems through these photographs. How is that possible I hear you ask? Well, this is one of my favourite subjects but I will try to be brief because unless you are going to take up healing you really don't need to know it all and it could fill a book all on its own.

All through the universe there are crisscrossing lines of energy and these are duplicated on our planet. We call them ley lines and where many of these lines cross our ancestors believed there were very powerful energies at these points. Because of this belief these were the places they erected standing stones, stone circles and later, places of worship. Haven't we all sometimes wondered just why a certain church was built where it was? Well, I may have just given you the answer. These lines are easily detected by dowsers. Even I have done it, so that proves it isn't difficult. In other parts of the world these "special" places are used in different ways, but man has always known of them.

These lines of energy are reflected yet again around the human body and again where many lines cross we have vortices of energy. We call these chakras (the Sanskrit word for wheels) or energy centres, depending on your Eastern or Western culture, but there are other names for them as well. There are seven major centres just outside the physical body and linking in to the endocrine glands within the body. There are very many more minor ones but for healing purposes we concentrate on the major ones. The first of these is level with the base of the spine and this I know to be a vibrant red, I'll explain more later in the chapter on colour, then we have another one at the sacral area, it is orange, next is the solar plexus – yellow, heart – green, throat – blue, forehead or third eye – indigo and crown of the head – violet. These centres spin and the energy from them in the form of colour is what is seen as the aura. When this is photographed, experts in this field can tell a great deal by the colours shown to be around us. Some colours may be in abundance and others lacking. Briefly a shortage of red may suggest tiredness and lack of energy. This is a very tiny example of what I am referring to. This field of healing is fascinating and later my colour therapy training was to open many more doors for me in this respect.

CHAPTER 7

HEALING "HANKIES"

Back in the early days of my spiritual development Bob, my friend and healing mentor, had told me a few times that if I was ever in need of help and couldn't make a trip up to Stonehaven to see him in person, he would send me distant healing. The first time he said this I didn't ask any questions because I didn't want to show how completely ignorant I was on this subject, but I remember thinking "Aye, that'll be right". So, as can happen, and no doubt to take my education a step even further, the universe took a hand and sent me a really bad day. I woke feeling very ill, and there was no way I could miss work. At the time I was managing a small wool mill shop in the town and that week my only assistant was on holiday. When I had a minute to spare I phoned Bob asking for help. He said he would send healing at the first opportunity during his almost certainly equally busy day. This he did during his lunch break. In my job I was rushed right through until mid-afternoon when I found the time to grab a sandwich, a cup of tea and a sit down. Of course I was now not only still feeling ill but also totally exhausted. Finishing my sandwich in the privacy of the back shop,

I put my feet up, sat back and relaxed. Immediately I felt the healing energy sweep through my body. It felt exactly as it did when sitting in Bob's healing room. I was even sure I could feel his hands on my shoulders. I enjoyed this feeling for about ten minutes when, just as suddenly as the healing energy had arrived, it vanished. Did I imagine it? I don't think so for most of my pain, discomfort and exhaustion had vanished too. This was convincing enough for me. It's worth pointing out here that Bob had sent the healing energy two hours before I felt it! Another useful lesson for me was that in the healing world time just doesn't exist. From then on and indeed up until a short time ago, I practised distant healing for all my people every night without fail. I never specified an exact time for this (I am aware that some healers do) but nevertheless in many cases the people I was concentrating on could actually tell *me* when they were receiving it.

To help you understand how distant healing is possible, think again about this web of energy surrounding and interweaving with our universe, think of our complete connection to it, and through it to each other and even to those now in the spirit world. Remember too that I said that our thoughts can affect others. That was a difficult one for me to swallow and perhaps it is for you too. Far from trying to persuade you one way or the other I prefer to remind you of what I was continually told on my first visits to the spiritualist church, and that was to accept only what felt right for me at that time. I cannot give you better advice. I had to learn to crawl before I could walk and had I not had all this stuff given to me slowly bit by bit over a long period with proof that satisfied *me*, I could never have been comfortable with or accepting of any of it. Writing this book has been one of the most difficult challenges I have faced in my life. This has been somewhat due to the general climate around me of disbelief and even fear of the metaphysical or supernatural. But are these words not interchangeable with the word "divine"? I seem to remember that it was Jesus himself who said that what he could do we could all do. He did phrase it a little better than that I know! So why should healing be restricted in any way whatsoever? My purpose in putting in all the hard work (and for me it is *such* hard work) of sharing my experiences is to help, even if only a few of you, to consider that just possibly this could all be true. Maybe the world isn't flat after all! In the light of that I think you will all be ready for my next bit of sharing.

Not very long after developing this distant healing routine I read an interesting letter in the Psychic News. I did feel I was very daring to buy this newspaper and although I read it from cover to cover I kept it well hidden from prying eyes. What a hypocrite I must have been back then. This letter was from someone who did distant healing using squares of white cloth, the size of a hankie apparently. Well, what novice healer wouldn't be intrigued by that? As a compulsive stitcher, bits of cloth really appealed to me. This was familiar territory and I couldn't wait to try this out but none of my healing friends had heard of it (apart from reading the same article). Apparently I was on my own on this one, so how to start? First I tried different fabrics and quickly decided that an all natural fabric was best, so I settled for pure cotton. All I had to do it seemed was take the piece of cotton, hold it between my hands, tune in and channel the healing energy into the cloth, all as I would do with a person. This cloth was then placed in an envelope and given or sent to the person concerned. They then placed it on any part of their body, in a pocket or even under the sheet or pillow on their bed. No-one other than healer or person in need of it must be allowed to touch it. I later learned that another person could act as a surrogate for a child and in the months to come I found that these cloths under the sheet or pillow of a difficult or ill child were very beneficial.

I asked my very good friend Susie if she would help me with this experiment. I first met Susie, who had heard of me in a very roundabout way, early on in my healing career. She had breast cancer and because her mother and grandmother had both died of this, it was hard for her to shake off the belief that she would too. Although Susie had been given a maximum of two years to live and that was with all the medical help available at that time, we had a twelve year journey together and it was a huge privilege for me to help her and to have her as a friend.

The "extra" twelve years she had after diagnosis was due to her medical care (this was excellent), healthy eating, positive thinking as well as all the healing I could channel to her. Although Susie was an extremely positive thinker in all other ways she did always believe that her cancer was a family thing and that she would eventually die from it. Susie was the ideal person to help with my experiment and she was very enthusiastic and couldn't wait to try out her first "hankie" as she called it. And guess what? It worked! Over and over she found relief from her pain. Later, nearing the end of her life these hankies placed on her chest at night helped her get some rest from the pain that was gradually taking over her life in spite of her prescribed drugs.

Because I was now channelling healing into so many cloths for Susie and others, I thought I would experiment with a little mass production by projecting healing into three pieces of cotton at a time but folded together as one. This was purely to save a little time. Susie and I had discussed this beforehand. The first night using only one of the cloths Susie found no relief whatsoever. On returning from the bathroom in the middle of the night and quite desperate to get some sleep she noticed a strange warmth on the side of her face next to her little bedside table. On this table were lying the remaining two cloths. Susie was a very psychically aware person and intuitively she immediately placed all three cloths on her chest as one. As if by magic she told me later, the healing energy was there as before. Now I knew that each cloth had to be treated individually. I would never have worked that out but for Susie's intuition.

Another person I could trust to give honest feedback had been having healing for a severe pain in his chest. In spite of all the tests possible no reason for this pain could be found by the medical profession. I was a last resort he said. So nothing new there then I thought. Now as this man was a scientist, I felt he would not be easily influenced either way and, as I said, I could trust him to be totally honest with me. On explaining my experiment to him and asking for his help, he looked at me in sheer astonishment and said "For goodness sake Betty, I'm a scientist. Do you realise just how much mind searching I had to do before coming to someone like you in the first place, and then admitting that you are indeed helping me? This healing business goes against all my professional training and beliefs and now you ask me to take away a bit of cotton and expect me to wear it in a pocket to get the same benefit." But he did take it away and he did get the same healing from the cloth as through my hands. He actually told me that with the cloth tucked into the breast pocket of his shirt, it felt as if my hands were actually on his body. Now what do you think of that then? He told me too that his cloths being laundered cancelled the healing benefit. I probably could have worked that out for myself!

I now felt I could go forward with a bit more research. In particular I wanted to know how long the healing energy would continue to be felt. Now I am making no claims here, I am simply telling you what my people found. To my surprise I had no difficulty in finding people to test these cloths out on. The general opinion was that having found the courage to come to me in the first place they trusted me implicitly after that. Generally we found that the more ill a person was the shorter time the cloth "worked". With the less ill the longer the benefit lasted.

Gradually over a period of time the requests for "Betty's healing hankies" as some people called them, increased until I found I was sending them all over the country. After a time I found I was spending more and more time sitting alone in my healing room with bits of white cotton between my hands and my intuition told me it was time to call a halt. Remember too I couldn't mass produce. Each cloth had to be treated separately and I much preferred the one to one human contact. But it was a very interesting experiment to do and because of the steadily growing number of requests I considered it very worthwhile at the time, but we should all listen to our inner guidance and mine was telling me to move on.

However these experiments did prove to me just how wondrous healing could be, and made it much easier for me to accept so much of what knowledge was yet to come my way. I really did come to believe that all things are possible.

CHAPTER 8

MEDITATION

(or a little time out!)

Very early on in my healing career I was introduced to meditation. To develop as a healing channel, regularly practising meditation is almost essential. But if only we would all get into the habit of meditating regularly I truly believe we would change our lives for the better and it need not cost a penny, just a little time and a lot of dedication to stick to it.

Although my purpose in meditating was to improve my healing channelling abilities, I quickly realised how many of my people could benefit from this too. I started recording my own visualisation/meditation tapes to help those I knew who would benefit from them. The feedback I got from my first tapes (no CD's then) was very positive and this gave me the confidence to expand them further.

At one point one of my people was involved in forming a group called the Angus Cancer Support Group and, because she was already using my tapes herself, she asked me if I would make a selection especially for members of this group to borrow. Of course I was willing and I enlisted the help of my friend Susie who had helped with my healing cloths experiment and, as I was now seeing quite a number of other cancer sufferers, I asked for their input too. I heeded all their suggestions when making these tapes. I had been learning a good deal too about other ways to help people and flower remedies came out near the top with them. So, on the reverse side of each tape I recorded a talk on the Bach Flower Remedies (more info on these later) and some information on which ones had been found to be beneficial by others depending on their state of mind at any particular time. As the content of each tape was my own I asked that they be freely copied and shared.

I was also asked if I could recommend any books for patients and again I enlisted Susie's help and that of others too, in making up a list of all books that they had found useful and beneficial. The organisers of the Angus Cancer Support Group were particularly keen to have the benefit of the experiences of those who had already travelled this path.

After a time this group was replaced by the MacMillan Centre and I so admire the work they do, but it was also such a privilege to be asked to help in the first instance. That group was started around 1991/2 and the progress made since then in patient support is phenomenal.

So now for those of you who haven't given this form of relaxation a try I will explain a little. I can so thoroughly recommend it. You will benefit from even ten minutes a day. Skip this bit if you happen to be a balanced, happy, worry free individual, or if you are already an experienced meditator.

For the rest of you I suggest you start by focussed daydreaming. We can all do that and indeed some of us spend a considerable time doing it. People who daydream a lot are said to be very relaxed and content. So give yourself permission to relax and see yourself walking on a beach, through a wood carpeted with wild flowers or see yourself doing anything, being any place, that gives you pleasure. Keep that up for a whilie.

Now we go one step further. You have been "seeing yourself" doing all this, now try *being* in your own body doing it. Instead of watching yourself you will now be sensing, smelling the sea, feeling the texture of the tree bark under your fingers, the softness of grass or sand beneath your feet, and the warmth of the sun on your face, all without moving from your chair. It's a ten minute pick me up. How good and easy is that then?

Now that is visualisation in its simplest form. This can be taken much further by visualising happy resolutions to any problems you may have for instance, it doesn't work too well for seeing yourself winning the lottery by the way, but it may help for other things. There are really good books on this and the subject of meditation, and if this tiny glimpse has grabbed your attention then I strongly suggest you find a good teacher or a book on the subject. I am a great believer in the saying "If you can perceive it, you can achieve it". Mind, one ten minute session is unlikely to land you the job of your dreams. You will have to put in a little more effort than that. This is the dedication bit I referred to earlier.

A few words now on meditation. I explained way back in Chapter 3 about the vibrational levels of the brain and when you really enter into the visualisation thing your level will slip from Beta (our everyday living level remember) into the Alpha level. The aim for most people in meditation is to slip even further into Theta. This does usually take quite a lot of practice unless you are one of the lucky ones and it comes naturally. There are many ways of course of achieving this state and it is greatly helped by being in a group, as long as it is led by an experienced person. This is very important. However to share my own preferred method, I choose music that relaxes *me*, after listening to this for a short period I allow my mind to slip into a state where I no longer hear the music, and I find myself in this wonderful state of just "being". Nothing in my head and I am unaware of my surroundings. Thoughts may slip into my mind now and again – like what's for supper tonight or did I remember to…. this is OK, I just let them slip away and give them no concentration whatsoever. Others like to sit and concentrate on a candle flame, a flower or sometimes repeating words like "peace". All are fine, it's the state of mind you want to get into, and the journey there is personal to you. Nothing is right, nothing is wrong, it just is.

At one point I taught an evening class in "Meditation and Natural Therapies" and I had planned all ten weeks of this class very carefully. The saying "The best laid plans etc." comes to mind here. The first forty minutes of the two hour session I had planned a short visualisation/meditation followed by discussion. Then I would do a short talk on therapies suitable and safe for using at home.

The visualisations/meditations I had also planned in detail as follows –first few weeks, a simple visualisation and I led this as a walk through a garden, into a meadow, on into a wood and down to a beach where I would remain silent and leave my students to hopefully achieve a state of meditation. I really thought this would appeal to everyone. Now leading visualisations is fraught with problems and in leading this group I found that one person didn't like the garden because she was scared of bees and wasps, another didn't fancy the meadow because she got hay fever and yet another was badly affected by tree pollen. Well this certainly showed that I was doing something right for they were all truly taking themselves to another place! This is exactly why a group must be led by an experienced person. The last few weeks of the classes I had planned that I would remain silent, as everyone would have reached a point where they could visualise on their own. In reality it turned out that for the full ten weeks in every class I taught, and they went on for a few years, all the students wanted to be led through the visualisation and some stayed in the garden and reached a state of meditation, others carried on to the meadow or the wood and yet others to the beach. But no-one wanted to go it alone and I had been so looking forward to a few nights of silence on my part! What did please and surprise me greatly though was the fact that these visualisations were so real to them that the thoughts of bees and pollen came into their minds at all. Done properly visualisation can be a very powerful means to inner peace and positive outcomes.

One evening I led the class into a state of relaxation and then deeper for the purpose of sending healing to anyone they knew who was in need of it. This was meant to be a gentle introduction to distant healing as the lecture to follow was on this subject. One lady thought of a relative who was in a wheelchair and in her mind she travelled to the home of this person, and again in her mind brought them back to the room we were in to share in the healing energy. This journey of course was unnecessary as her thoughts would have sufficed. Maybe I didn't explain this well enough. After a time I said we had completed the healing and that I was going to bring them back slowly to the Beta level. If you have been on a journey somewhere this is best done by retracing all steps arriving back at the place you started from. Well, this lady panicked and hastily in her mind returned her invalid relative to his home and then still all in her mind hurried back again to our room. When she finally opened her eyes we were all astonished to find her breathing very heavily and looking quite put out. On asking her if she was all right she told us of the rush she had making this journey! This just proved the point I had been trying to make of just how powerful visualisations and meditations can be – even simple ones. So much so that it's essential to feel you are properly grounded after this experience and this is best done by being aware of your feet on the floor or the ground. A cup of tea helps greatly too.

Meditation now is a little different but can follow on from visualisation if this is preferred. In visualisations we are always aware of our surroundings and they can be exactly what we see them to be, but in meditation we must reach a deeper level of relaxation until we are completely unaware of anything except this wonderful feeling of just "being". We can be helped by people experienced in this field to achieve this but by far the biggest part of getting there is daily practice.

There is a third step after visualisation and meditation and it is contemplation. I believe to achieve this state, much practice and support is needed over a long period of time, sometimes for years. I am not qualified to give any guidance on this one, but felt I would like to mention it.

CHAPTER 9

SOME UPS AND DOWNS OF

HEALING

After gaining much experience of healing at home I was asked to join the Church of the Spirit healing team on Thursday evenings. I considered this quite a privilege. Channelling healing within the church was quite different to working in my own home. O.K. the procedure was the same but everyone who came for healing in the church really believed it would work. Belief in anything is paramount if we are to succeed in it. Another factor was that when a few healers work together the energy in that space is much greater than the sum of its parts. Then too at the church, people came at the first sign of dis-ease and indeed many came for regular "top-ups". Of course we were always mindful that, when necessary, they had to be encouraged to see their doctor. In some cases we insisted that they do so. All healers in that church belonged to one of two organisations so we were very strictly regulated. We wouldn't have had it otherwise. Before I started doing healing work there was very little regulation in this field and I don't think it would have

89

Betty Fotheringham

occurred to any of us that we would need insurance. It wasn't just that we were a trusting lot, it was more a case of what could we possibly do wrong? We didn't manipulate joints nor did we do any massage, so how could there be a problem? However times change and gradually we came to realise that we needed credentials and having got our relevant "bits of paper", Certificates of Competence in other words, it was then possible to get insurance cover.

Although I did appreciate the atmosphere while healing with others in the Church I felt I gained much more experience working in my little healing room at home. There was time for instance to let people talk and share their feelings in private. This was so valuable in different ways and in certain circumstances. All my people too were so happy, sometimes eager, to help when I wanted to carry out any research. Later, when I came to teach healing, this was all so good for sharing.

At one particular time I had three or four married couples coming to see me on a regular weekly basis. In every instance only the wife wanted healing, the men declaring that they were perfectly healthy. Although I preferred only the person seeking help to be in my healing room, obviously I didn't object to a happily married couple staying together when they requested this. Of course I did have to be careful, because if the husband was pushy about sitting in, *he* may just have been part of his wife's problem. That didn't happen often and I think initially the wives were looking for a bit of support from their husbands, because there was no doubt when I started on this healing journey, it was definitely regarded as weird or spooky, as was I! It was my job to set minds at rest with a full explanation of how healing worked and what to expect.

But, to the great surprise of all, these perfectly healthy men, (or so they claimed) found that, as the healing energy I was channelling filled the small room, they too were receiving it in full measure. They all loved this and found that aches and pains they had been ignoring for some time all cleared up and I hadn't even touched them. Of course to me there was no mystery about this and jokingly we all came to refer to it as "twofors". Two for the price of one in other words. But happenings such as these did a great deal to prove just how powerful healing could be.

Another interesting story concerned Frank and his office colleagues. As I have already said Frank had no hesitation in telling people I was a healer and at some point he must have told his colleagues down in Kent. Frank worked from home but there had to be daily telephone contact with the office down south. No mobiles or emails back then. This call usually took place when the office opened at 9 a.m. but Frank had often left long before then and I would have to take the calls. No-one from the office ever mentioned healing to me at any time but I noticed they did like to chat and share their problems. I have no doubt I had sympathised with them, although I have little recollection of this.

On Frank's retirement he went south for a dinner and presentation and was told a rather strange tale. First he was told they were going to miss him, that was nice and understandable, but then he was told that they would miss me too and what were they going to do without me? I had only met a few of them briefly at a weekend "jolly" but apparently quite by chance the boys had found that if they were under the weather, had a pain or an injury, and if they got me on the phone instead of Frank, and if they told me all about their problem, they would miraculously (their word, not mine!) feel much better. It got that when any of them had a health problem they vied for who was going to phone Frank that day, and they would leave the call until they were sure he would have already left, so that they could speak to me!

I'm sure you will all have worked out what was happening here. And yes, I would have sent distant healing to them on hearing of their problems. But I am positive that the biggest factor here was their own belief that just talking to a healer would help them. The oftener betterment occurred for any of them the stronger this belief would become. Another bit of proof of the power of our own minds and a bit for distant healing as well.

Another point I would mention here was that I quickly learned that healing wasn't always the answer. Fortunately I was able to keep my feet on the ground and not get carried away by it all. In one instance someone who badly needed an eye operation came to see me, as he had been told that this was not possible at that time because of another medical condition. This gentleman turned out to be an ideal candidate for healing. His body absorbed the energy very easily, probably due to his completely open mind. After about three visits he went for a pre-booked check-up and his consultant was very surprised at the change in his eye and asked him what he had been doing. It transpired that the eye was now quite suitable for surgery. Now this was a perfect example of healing and medicine working together for the benefit of the patient. Other instances like this happened many times over the years and I felt privileged to be part of that. Oh, that this joining together of allopathic medicine and alternative therapies could be the norm.

There was another side too of course to healing in my own home. I did get quite a number of people who referred to me as their "last resort". They weren't necessarily convinced that I could help them, but they were very desperate and often said they would try *anything* to get well. At one point my husband threatened in jest to have a house sign made naming our home "The Last Resort". Attitude makes a huge difference when receiving healing as it does in every other area of life, and I did seem to be working against negative attitudes at least some of the time. We didn't see so much of this in the church. I came to dread the greeting, all so common, of "Betty, you're my last resort". Fortunately after a couple of visits people realised the value and benefit of what I offered and thoroughly appreciated all that could be done for them with healing.

Apart from initially listening carefully when each person seeking help shares their problems, healers gather information in different ways about any area of the body requiring treatment, and they may even be aware of the deeper cause of the person's complaint or illness. I cannot speak for others, but when I started on this healing career, I would know which area of the body to treat because I would get a tingle in that part of my own body. This frequently happened immediately on the person's arrival and before they had a chance to tell me anything. So, on feeling a twinge in my right knee say, by placing my hands on or near the person's right knee, I, and more importantly the person concerned, would feel heat, coolness or a tingling sensation. This was always a sure sign that the healing energy was flowing through me to the person. Very soon though I no longer came to need these physical "messages" I would just "know" the cause of the problem or in the case of injuries I might get an impression of a fall or wrench – something like that.

These insights were always confirmed later by the person receiving healing and some might say that getting information in this way made me a medium. I would have to agree with this for a medium is simply a channel between the different vibrational levels. I was absolutely open to any help with my healing, always being very careful of what I shared with the patients. Less was always best as we are not allowed to diagnose, nor would any of us wish to. Incidentally I can't now call anyone a patient – they have to be referred to as clients. This is just in case people get the impression that I think I am a doctor! As if! I'm not supposed to wear a white coat either for the same reason. I don't really look my best in white anyway. So no worries there.

Things didn't always go smoothly healing in my own home though. I had set up one of our bedrooms as a healing room. This room had a bed settee in it so that it could double as a bedroom when the need arose, but I was always conscious that other therapists had couches for their rooms. I neither had the space for one nor could I afford one, mainly because I refused to charge any more than a nominal sum for healing and even that was waived a lot of the time. I was happier with a small donation. In one case I was paid weekly with a beautiful home baked cream sponge. That suited me just fine and I never did let on that I didn't eat cream sponges as cream gives me migraines.

One day I had a brilliant idea (or so it seemed at the time), instead of a couch I would use my sun lounger from the summerhouse. Patients could sit and chat while it was in the upright position, then lift the arms to extend it full length with the person lying down for the actual healing. What could be simpler? The first guinea pig to try this out was a man I hadn't met before. How foolish was that then? All went very well until it came time for this gentleman to leave, when we found that he was stuck really fast in this chair. I hadn't allowed for really portly people you see. It took a lot of very embarrassing pushing and pulling to free him and it was no surprise that I never saw him again. The lounger was returned to my summerhouse pretty quickly and we were back to an upright chair again. I wasn't sure how my insurance company would look at a claim for damages of this nature and clearly too I would have to up my game a bit.

Another incident that comes equally clearly to mind was one of my "last resorters." I will call this person Heather and she came to see me on the recommendation of another of my people because her family was at their wits' end to know what to do with her.

The alarm bells clanged inside my head as Heather told me her tale. Doctors, consultants, acupuncturists, osteopaths – they had all come and gone I was told, and I fancy on their part, quickly and thankfully. I secretly wondered how long I would last and, rather uncharacteristically for me, I hoped that it would not be very long. Heather had a leg problem that defied all medical knowledge to diagnose or treat – or so she said. The doctors no doubt were being tactful. "Betty, they can't make anything of me", said Heather proudly. Now I had heard the expression "so and so enjoys ill health" used from time to time and I had always thought this rather a peculiar one. After meeting Heather (and there were others too) I understood completely the meaning of the word "enjoy" used in this context. I already knew that my time with Heather was not going to be my finest hour. Getting at last down to the business side of things, she asked if I made a charge, knowing full well that I did as we had discussed it on the phone before she came. With great courage I repeated the figure already agreed upon. Compared to other therapists this was very small indeed. A massive stroke was only just avoided by a quick reduction. May I say here that Heather was very much in the minority with this attitude to healers. Only a very few told me that I had a gift from God and that I should work for nothing. The majority of my people continually told me that I needed to revise my charges upwards.

Betty Fotheringham

As Heather's treatment commenced her bad leg rose some two feet into the air. I only needed to move near that side of her body and up it went, lowering itself gently to the floor as I moved away. I was almost tempted to play tricks on it and sneak round unnoticed. We healers are quite accustomed to remarkable happenings. "Weird" to others is commonplace to us, but this was not a remarkable happening, this was Heather milking it for all her worth. She kept exclaiming "My Betty, what power you have, just look at my leg, I can't do a thing with it". A bit like a bad hair day, I thought. I wanted to say "What a vivid imagination you have Heather", but we healers have a Code of Conduct and it's a bit restrictive when it comes to telling our clients what we really think of them in circumstances such as this. I struggled on with her for a few weeks, getting absolutely nowhere. The leg still rose as if on a pulley every time I approached, and according to Heather, I "wasn't doing much for her". No surprises there then. Sometimes I got paid a tiny fee, most often not for various reasons. Then, instead of appearing for her appointment one day, I got a frantic phone call – she couldn't walk, she was absolutely paralysed, would I come? Not likely I thought, this was the chance I had been waiting for. I gently pointed out to her that her doctor's surgery was quite near her home and suggested so kindly, that she should call him in.

Since I now had an hour to spare, I had a quick cup of tea and set off to do some much needed shopping. Who should I be following in the supermarket with her trolley? You've guessed it, Heather of course. She spotted me behind her and set off at a cracking pace. Later, on the way home in my car, I nearly bumped into her again. She was in the middle of the street right in front of me. Even healers are human and my halo nearly slipped, I was sorely tempted to accelerate, but just in time I remembered my Code of Conduct. No Brownie points for running down one of my people so I braked smartly and with a hop, skip and a jump Heather was safely on the pavement. I never saw her again. Thank you God

Sometimes people had to travel to see me by bus and although there is a bus stop at the end of my street, it was the times of the buses that presented me with problems. I must be one of the few healers who perfected the length of healing appointments to fit in with bus time tables. Not for me an appointment on the hour or half hour – it was more like "Please may I have an appointment for 10.36 and I really need to catch the next bus at 11.20?" One couple had to travel on three buses to visit me and another three to get back home. I found them very interesting in some ways, but they presented a fairly steep learning curve for me in others. These two were brother and sister who had lost their partners and now shared a home. Let's call them

Mr W and Mrs C. No informality here, unlike all my other people who were more than glad to shorten a mouthful like Mrs Fotheringham to just Betty. Normally, after a couple of visits, people would come into my home, give me a hug and address me as "Betty", but with Mr W and Mrs C we would formally shake hands in welcome, usually while they were still standing on my doorstep, and I was addressed very respectfully as Mrs Fotheringham. I was far more comfortable with the exuberant hugs.

Perhaps I should just add here that our training always advised extreme caution when seeing people in our own home. As a woman I only ever saw men for the first few appointments at times when my husband was in the house. Over many years of working from home I never once had any reason to feel unsafe. The help I could give just didn't attract that kind of person.

Mrs C had told me on the phone that she was deaf and had bad knees. Mr W had very bad arthritis in his feet and was reduced to wearing very old black lacing gym shoes. (Remember them anyone?) These, he complained, were all he could bear on his feet and he hobbled along in them obviously in great discomfort. On their first visit I saw them approach from a distance and it was clear to me that they were arguing hotly about something, and it seemed as if Mr W had the upper hand. I later learned I was the subject of the argument. They each had a preconceived opinion of what I would look and be like. Much later again I was told that they found on meeting me that they were both wrong. Apparently I turned out to be respectable, relatively young, no crystal ball and very professional. They spared my feelings by not telling me what they *had* expected – I was grateful for that small mercy.

This couple knew very little of healing or healers. They had been given my name by my healing federation, and perhaps because they knew nothing of what was likely to take place, they initially chose to come into my healing room together, safety in numbers I expect, but it was quickly apparent that this wasn't going to work. Mr W was definitely not going to let Mrs C get a word in. I didn't usually encourage two or more people in my healing room for this very reason. In the case of a child of course it was obligatory for a parent to be present. I did make an exception for twofors as I explained earlier.

I quickly split this rowing couple up and wasn't surprised to find that the lady not only had a very bad knee problem, but her deafness was extreme. No real surprises there. I probably would have been deaf too if I'd had to live with her bossy argumentative brother for any length of time. She had all my sympathy. My interest in the *causes* of health issues led me to spend the first part of a consultation exploring what was going on around someone's health problem. More on this later. For instance in Mrs C's case deafness led me to ask what was in her life that she didn't want to hear. It was fairly obvious in this case but it isn't always so. Healing would be of limited benefit unless the circumstances around her changed or she changed her attitude to them. This was a part of my healing work that I found very fascinating and I loved to let people talk through their own problems and reach their own conclusions. To allow them to work out a probable cause of their difficulties for themselves, was so much more valuable than me suggesting possibilities to them. I frequently had to very gently make people aware of the now accepted fact, that we are unlikely to heal if we continue living in the same environment that caused the problem in the first place. This often boils down to simply changing our thinking towards whatever is making us ill. You'll be glad to know we don't necessarily have to move house. That's not what I mean about environment! There is an upside and a downside to everything on this planet and that includes us and every circumstance we find ourselves in. It's sad that so many of us humans seem to focus on the negative. And aren't we hard going to those around us when we do this, for we lower their vitality as well as our own. As healers we are lucky to be taught early on in our training how to protect ourselves from such negativity, but we do have to work at it, and it does give us the experience we need to help others in a similar situation.

Let's get back to Mrs C's bad knees. This made me wonder if her brother's attitude sometimes "brought her to her knees". On the other hand Mr W's feet were so badly affected by arthritis that he couldn't wear shoes and could only hobble about, and this suggested to me that he was afraid of change and moving on. It was the feet bit that gave me the possible clue here, and, as I had discovered even at our first meeting, he was very critical. These two were so jealous of each other that I divided my time meticulously between them and played soft music (different for each) to help them relax. That was my first mistake with Mr W, he didn't like his music and said so peevishly – it reminded him too much of his youth and that made him feel sad. Another clue here perhaps? At the next visit he told me that his sister didn't like hers either, so I swapped the music round and thankfully that solved that little problem. Mr W insisted on having his healing session first. He held the unshakeable belief that the energy would all be used up if his sister went before him! I was really going to have to mind my P's and Q's here.

With me Mrs C was a gentle sweet appreciative person and we got along famously. After a time though her hearing had only marginally improved, and I didn't expect much more as I could hardly tell her to ditch her brother. Mr W made me aware in no uncertain terms that I was doing him no good whatsoever and when was I going to start actually "healing" him? He was one of the very, very few people who could not feel any healing energy at all while I was working with him. I got the same complaint from him week after week. Eventually I felt obliged to point out that he could now wear his leather shoes quite comfortably and was actually walking normally, or he did so when he thought I couldn't see him! On quietly observing him approaching my home I noticed that his walking deteriorated the nearer he got to my house until he was back to hobbling up my steps and in the door. However, I changed my healing routine with him and started to massage his feet while channelling the healing energy and he was content. He said he now felt I was actually *doing* something for him. Woe is me. (These two people by the way have long gone otherwise I would not be telling this tale.)

The siblings continued to argue their way up to my house for some weeks. They argued over my age, how many children I had, how old they were likely to be, how old my husband was likely to be, what he did for a living, and so on and on. I found all this out because now and then Mrs C would ask me these things declaring that she was only asking because her brother wanted to know!

Mrs C enjoyed her visits tremendously and she said she loved the peace and quiet of my home. Mr W didn't apparently enjoy any of it and told me frequently that this was so. He quickly added that he didn't want to stop coming though. He magnanimously wanted to give me a fair chance he said. Inevitably the time came for Mrs C's visits to stop. She was very sad about this, but her knees had completely recovered and we both agreed that her deafness was not responding. It was decided that Mr W would come by himself for a few more weeks. (Lucky me, I thought.) That night the phone rang, it was a very agitated Mrs C and she told me she had fallen getting off the third bus on her way home and had hurt her knees again, could she possibly come for just another few weeks. She also said she would miss her "lovely days out" and her hour in the peace and tranquillity of my home. Well it wasn't too difficult to work out what was going on here, but I did make sure that they finally finished their visits simultaneously. The lesson I took from all this was to make sure that in future none of my people became too dependent on their healing "fixes". I certainly didn't want to be the excuse for any other "lovely days out". I learned a huge amount more about the possible causes of ill health from working with and observing this couple, and as I said, I give some other examples of this aspect of healing later in the book.

CHAPTER 10

PENDULUM POWER

I mentioned earlier that while living on the croft as a child, my father introduced me to dowsing. I would have been about nine or ten at the time. On the croft all our water for the house came from a well and this was always full of lovely cool clear water. For the animals when they were out in the fields, we had to rely on rainwater to fill the burns or ditches that ran alongside each field, and in the summer months this could present a problem. We did have water troughs here and there but transporting water to these was a real nuisance. One particularly hot dry summer Dad feared that the burns were going to dry up, and he decided that we would dowse to locate any underground springs, "Just in case" he said. I'm not sure just how much he really knew about dowsing or what experience he actually had, but any lack of know-how never stopped my Dad from doing anything he set his mind to. I consider myself hugely fortunate to have inherited that belief. His expression of "If ye set yer mind tult ye can dae onything" lives on with me as "If I think I can, then I can". Or if you prefer it in the words of one of the famous, Henry Ford put it as "If you think you can, if you think you can't, either way you are

106

right." Now I'm sure you have all got my message so let's get back to this dowsing business. Dad cut each of us a forked hazel twig, just to get us started, promising us something better when we had more experience. Apparently, according to my fount of all knowledge, as my Dad was for me at that age, as hazel trees grew abundantly in or near water it was the ideal tree to use if we were dowsing *for* water. Many years on I learned that this was indeed true.

My mother, my sister Gladys and I were far from keen on this experiment, but humoured Dad just the same. Our brief instructions from him were to pace the field holding the two points of our twig, and keeping a little tension on them. We had to look out for any movement of it. Our joint scepticism was at a high level, except for Dad of course. After a very few minutes though, my sister's twig jerked upwards nearly hitting her face. "Beginner's luck" Dad said, "Try again". At her second attempt over the same spot, Gladys could barely hold her twig, the movement was so strong. She panicked, threw it in the air and ran back to the house, vowing never to touch a dowser again. It was just too spooky she said. Having seen this performance by Gladys I was now very keen for some response from my twig. I reckoned I could handle spooky. Disappointingly my mother and I had no response whatsoever from our dowsers that day. My father, thanks to his own ability and that of Gladys (brief though that was), had found his water and we never did need it for as usual for the rest of that summer it rained aplenty.

Now come forward a bit in time with me by some years for my life of getting married, living in a city and bringing up children, didn't leave much time for interests like dowsing, and when I needed water I could always turn on a tap! But now here I was enquiring into all sorts of believe it or not things or spooky wae o' daens as some of them seemed to me, and because of that experience with my Dad my interest in dowsing was rekindled. Now in everything I have explored over the years I have always tried as far as possible to get professional training, and on this occasion I was lucky enough to get a place on a weekend dowsing course taught by a very well-known and highly experienced healer. It was a big class and I knew no-one else there. I'm not at my best in these circumstances. To add to my discomfort I didn't shine in a dowsing sense that weekend either, but I was hooked forever. The lectures were excellent and I soaked up all the information like a sponge. My let down came during the practice sessions when, as on the croft, I could get no response whatsoever from my dowser. Of course I was no longer using Dad's bit of twig, instead I had angle-rods made from two old metal coat hangers and a little pendulum made by attaching a heavy glass bead to a length of thread. The coat hangers were the ones from the dry cleaners. "Use what you have and you'll never want" was another old family motto. My Mum and Dad were full of such sayings and boringly no doubt sometimes, so am I. Anyway where I lived pendulum shops were thin on the ground and I saw no need to go daft and buy when I could easily make.

In spite of my apparent lack of success, this course for me was a real start to dowsing properly, but I did approach my teacher on the second day to ask why I was having no success with either bead or coat hanger. He informed me that there was a simple explanation for this. Although he could have known absolutely nothing about me, he told me that as I was a natural healer I didn't need either the pendulum or the rods. All I had to do I was told was "tune in", ask my question, and I would get the answer, either through my hands or it would simply drop into my mind. Now, at that time I thought this was a real cop out as I had paid rather a large sum of money for that weekend and I felt a bit cheated because of my lack of progress. To be fair, to a crofter's daughter almost any sum of money is viewed as large, and this course cost only a little above the going rate at that time. But that weekend was another lesson for me in developing a less judgemental attitude because I had all the lecture notes, I bought a book for beginners and in no time at all I had mastered dowsing. Of course that was only the start, for I still had to gain experience and that takes time and dedication. I did come to realise that my healing intuition could indeed have given me lots of the answers I was seeking, but that training weekend I just wanted to be like everyone else and see my little pendulum dancing around on its short thread.

Dowsing can be used in many diverse situations. For instance, as on the croft, to find underground water, but it is also the easiest method of finding water or gas pipes, electricity cables, drains and such like coming into properties where any plans don't show these clearly. Or, as in many cases, the plans may have been lost over the years. Dowsing can save a lot of expensive digging in the wrong places. Country people in the past, and perhaps it is still so today, would always have turned to a dowser first to locate any underground problems they may have had, and anyone with dowsing ability was treated with great respect. I've just realised that I never knew of any ladies who dowsed professionally in this field. Why would that be I wonder? Perhaps it was nothing more than that imaginary line that used to be drawn between what was considered a suitable occupation for a woman and that for a man. But we still have plenty of highly skilled people working in this area of dowsing or divining, and the angle-rods are mostly used here, as, if using a pendulum outdoors, it may be affected by even a gentle breeze. Another advantage of angle-rods is that compared to a pendulum, they cannot easily be influenced by the mind. This use of the rods is still not one of my areas of expertise, probably simply because I never use them for this purpose. However after doing another course studying geopathic stress and earth energies, I am able to use my rods to check out my house and garden every now and then. It is common knowledge in most parts of the world that some buildings are unhealthy due possibly to underground running water, sometimes referred to as black streams, or certain minerals in the ground, but there are other causes too. I'm not going into more detail on that aspect of dowsing because this is a highly skilled area and I do not consider myself qualified in this, and there are plenty of people who are. I did find though that my study of geopathic stress served me well some years on and I would like to share this interesting experience with you.

At the time in question I had been visiting someone in his own home for a lengthy period of time. Tom (not his real name of course) had been diagnosed some time before with a terminal illness. He was a very brave man who never complained and I came to hugely admire and respect him and his wife. Tom and I often discussed possible reasons for his illness as he knew of my interest in this aspect of healing. I had by then devoted quite a bit of my time to reading much of what had been written on the causes of different health issues, and Tom's case just did not fit in to any of it. I had also read up on some causes of "sick building syndrome" because of certain other people I was helping at that time with another illness.

Now each time I had visited Tom in his own home I had a "feeling" about the house (very beautiful though it was) and I was very curious about the behaviour of their cat. Yes, that *is* what I said. This cat chose exactly the same spot on the floor to sleep, although this spot appeared to me to be the most unlikely place for any animal to settle. I had been brought up with so many animals around me that their different behaviours were very familiar to me. One week on visiting Tom, the furniture had been moved around and a settee now covered the cat's favoured place on the floor. But there it was fast asleep perched awkwardly, if indeed a cat can ever look awkward, along the back of this settee and exactly over its previously preferred spot. This gave me the clue I needed. I had been told that any bad energy spots in a house will be avoided by dogs but sought out and claimed by cats. Now I didn't know for certain if this story was true or not, but my feelings about the house were strong enough for me to share all I knew about geopathic stress with Tom, and suggested that he post off plans of the layout of his home to a very reputable and trustworthy dowser in London that I knew of, and had been helped by previously. This man, who specialised in this area of dowsing, found a bad energy line running beneath the house and a strong point directly on the spot where the cat chose to sleep. This is another one of my believe it or not stories and sadly of course this discovery could make no difference to Tom's situation, if indeed it ever had any bearing on his illness and I certainly make no claim to this whatsoever. It did mean though that they were able to change the children's sleeping areas – just in case. My contact in London made no charge for this service. I enlisted this man's help and expertise a few times over the years. Each expert in this field of dowsing has their own method of dealing with these energies if they are harmful, but this area of dowsing really should be left to them.

Now you may be a little surprised that this man dowsed over a plan of a house in Angus from his office in London, but "scouts' honour" this is for real. Indeed I have often read of dowsers, also working from their home or office, using this distant method, with maps of course, to find oil and various minerals in different parts of the world. It is possible too to buy hollow pendulums and into those can be placed a little of whatever the dowser wants to locate. This apparently ensures greater success. It was on learning of this that I realised why my Dad was right to choose hazel twigs for our first attempts at finding water on the croft. If we can just keep an open mind this can be a fascinating world to live in.

Returning to my own experience with a pendulum I needed lots of practice before I felt I was proficient, and I consider I am still learning. I did find that I could easily get more than a simple "yes/no" answer to any question. For instance if I ask my pendulum for a simple "yes/no" answer it will swing or rotate and for me a clockwise rotation is a yes answer, but this may vary from person to person. A "no" answer for me is a diagonal swing. An anticlockwise rotation indicates a "yes/but" reply and an opposite diagonal swing a "no/but". From this you will see that how you ask the question is of the utmost importance. When my pendulum goes on a sit down strike and refuses to move, this tells me to rephrase the question. I may have foolishly asked something like "Is it going to be a wet or dry day tomorrow?" Instead I should have asked if it is going to rain, will it rain all day or in the morning or in the afternoon? My first question can't have a "yes/no" answer but the others can. Before you start wondering, I have no interest in asking if I am going to win the lottery, but anything to do with health and well-being and I am on familiar territory. I may use my pendulum for checking to see if the tomatoes I have chosen in the supermarket have the residue of chemical sprays on them. Now I may get a "yes/but" answer to that so I would then ask, "Is this likely to be harmful to me?" My body is sensitive to some chemicals but not others and the level of spray may be too low to be harmful anyway. Can you see how it goes? It will also show you how wording that question as "Will these tomatoes harm me in any way?" would have given rise to a straight "yes" or "no" answer. Then, if say I feel a cold coming on I may dowse to check the vitamin C levels in my body and whether I need to boost them. If so would an orange a day suffice, or do I need to take a tablet. Getting our vitamins and minerals from our food is always preferable to taking supplements as there is less danger of overdosing, but this of course is assuming that there is sufficient vitamins and minerals in our food in the first place.

Other people can dowse to find missing objects very successfully. I am rubbish at that aspect of dowsing for some reason, probably again just because I don't practise it. Some dowsers even find missing people and I could go on and on for the human race has been dowsing in some form or another for thousands of years. We know this from cave paintings of figures holding dowsing tools.

After a time gaining much experience, I taught classes on dowsing and hopefully opened up another area of expertise for a lot of people, as I hope it will for you too. Of course instead of my coat hangers I now have a set of brass angle-rods, they are very businesslike, and I have a number of pendulums, my favourite being a beautiful crystal. I must now acknowledge that that teacher of long ago was right I *can* hold my hand over any substance and obtain the answers to my questions, and so I am careful not to let my little crystal rule my life. But it is a pleasure to have and to use.

If you feel you would like to explore dowsing further I suggest you find a good book, and there are many available. One I can recommend is by Arthur Bailey called *"Anyone can dowse for better health"* and then have a go. Thread a bead, a heavy washer or almost anything that comes to hand on to strong thread, cut the thread to about 5-6 inches in length initially just to get started, you can adjust the length to suit *you* when you have had a little practice. Sit or stand, relax, and simply ask your pendulum to give you a movement for "yes" and then one for "no". Accept the movements it makes without trying to influence them in any way. If your pendulum doesn't respond then gently swing it for a few seconds and then let it settle into its own choice of movement for a "yes" answer. With experience your pendulum will give answers without any prompting. Now that sounds easy doesn't it? All you have to do now is to spend some time practising. It is worth the effort, I promise you. Soon too you will reach the stage when you can influence your pendulum with your mind only. Now that's spooky so heed my cautionary words below.

<u>My cautionary words and other things to be careful of when learning.</u>

Dowsing, nor any of the therapies I speak of in this book, must not be used in place of a visit to your medical practitioner.

It is important to stay relaxed while dowsing, as being tense will almost certainly influence your results. Pendulums or angle-rods are simply amplifiers of our muscle reaction.

Do not use a pendulum for anything to do with health, your own or anyone else's until you have had plenty of experience. Always keep an open mind or perhaps, more accurately, keep a detached mind. As far as possible become a disinterested observer.

When practising dowsing avoid the presence of people who may have a negative attitude, either to dowsing or even just generally. Remember I said earlier how we are all connected and even our unspoken thoughts may affect others and vice versa. It is actually a good idea to avoid negative people at any time but sadly we do not always have that luxury!

Probably the most important thing of all is to be careful how you frame your questions. Initially ask only what can have a "yes/no" answer. Later you can move on to experimenting with "yes/but", "no/but" or "how many" and "for how long", but please learn to walk before you try to run. There's less likelihood then of tripping yourself up. Above all enjoy it!

Betty Fotheringham

CHAPTER 11

HOW I FOUND HOMEOPATHY, FLOWER REMEDIES and MUSCLE TESTING

Over many years I have explored, taken courses on and where possible, generally tried out many different therapies, all non-invasive and mostly energy based. Now just why have I done all this? Natural curiosity for a start, but more than anything it was due to my own health problems. Remember up until I got married I lived in the country on a croft. We ate our own organically produced food. The word "organic" was unknown to us by the way, for we knew of no other. The crops that we grew to feed ourselves, our hens and animals were all grown by crop rotation. Chemicals were either unobtainable or too expensive. Farmyard manure was preferred, as being a by-product on a farm it cost time only. We didn't have a lot of time but we had even less money.

It was a different world for me when, after getting married, I went to live in Edinburgh. Very quickly my body rebelled against the change. First I developed horrendous migraines, quickly followed by

118

all sorts of other nasties. My body I later discovered just couldn't take some of the highly processed foods I was now thoroughly enjoying. I had never had sausages from a butcher or pies from a baker before and with little skill in cooking then, I was taking full advantage of these new culinary delicacies! To be fair to myself, I was only eighteen and we still had food rationing. Our ration was one egg a week for instance, and for someone who had lived with hens all their life this was more than a little daunting. Then there were all the perfumes and chemicals in household cleaning products. The air, too, that I was breathing in the city was quite a contrast to that of the countryside. Even while at work in Stonehaven I was breathing fresh sea air and I still miss that after all these years.

But if I hadn't developed migraines, I wouldn't have met Bob, I wouldn't have experienced healing, and I wouldn't have become a healer. I consider migraines are a small price to pay for the years of channelling healing energy to so many people to their benefit. The eventual discovery of my intolerance to perfumes, household cleaners, North Sea gas, petrol etc. etc. has helped me to recognise the same problems in many other people. That too has been worth every day of illness I myself have had. I now find that with a few exceptions it is possible for me to stay well if I work at it a little.

All these challenges I faced in my own life led me first as I said into healing, but later into studying so many other therapies. After doing training in some of these things, I was able to share what I had learned with others. My aim has always been, if possible, to give people the tools or know how, so that they may help themselves to get well and then stay well. I was and still am aware too that healing is not for everyone. For some it is just too spooky in spite of all the evidence, for others it is perhaps not their time to let go of their illness, for they may still have to learn from it. Yes, our illnesses are always trying to tell us something and as this usually involves change, we can be mighty deaf when we don't want to hear. I know because I've been there.

Over the remaining chapters I would like to tell you of some of the exciting and interesting discoveries I have made over a lengthy period of time. Most of them fall into my believe it or not category, so some of you may struggle a little. These discoveries weren't all successes, some courses I took part in left little impression on me except for my purse. That brings me to where the money came from to pay for all this. First and foremost I had a very forbearing husband who supported me completely in all I did. He didn't understand some of it, wanted no part in it, but certainly approved of it all for me. In between my healing work, which at that time brought in next to no money, my own fault entirely, but to my regret I let myself be influenced by the few who came to me and told me that my healing was a "gift" from God and should be freely shared. So in between my healing work, I had a flower arranging business. This I ran conveniently from my home. At one time I shared three gardens growing most of my own flowers. That well-paying career ended abruptly when I became intolerant to the foam I used to build my arrangements. I also had to give up my teaching of evening classes in flower arranging. I tell you later how this intolerance was discovered. Another shove from the Universe? See what I mean? I have a qualification in Embroidery and Design so I changed over to teaching that and later Meditation and Natural Therapies. The Universe has a habit of whispering to us (more on this later) and nudges us in the right direction. If we turn a deaf ear then, as in my case, the whispers may become rather loud. There's nothing quite like having your means of earning taken from you to get your attention. When I was there it was very scary. I hadn't yet fully learned to trust in the Universe.

Due to my ever widening search for knowledge I had been picking up information here and there on homeopathy. Around that time too my body was getting more and more sensitive to prescribed drugs. For instance a consultant at our local hospital told me that another severe medical problem, I had was almost certainly a direct result of all the painkillers prescribed over a long period of time for migraine headaches. I had been on tranquilisers for these too to relieve stress. It was difficult for me to work out where all this stress was coming from for I was very happily married and had a normal family life. So why was I so stressed? My local doctor at that time (long since retired I may say) told me that the more tranquilisers he prescribed the less he saw of me. He also told me at the same time that I would probably live to a ripe old age and never know a day's wellness. Now that was fighting talk to me and I took it as a challenge to do more for myself. Could that just have been his motive, I wonder? Doctors are no fools. I did eventually learn to control my migraines through diet and avoiding certain chemicals in my home, but all that suffering didn't go to waste for it opened many avenues of learning for me. After all it was these debilitating headaches that put me on the path of healing and meeting my friend Bob in the first place. All the suffering was worth it for that alone, but here I was making other exciting discoveries such as the importance of our attitude to our problems. We are all on this earth to learn and we don't learn a lot when our lives are all plain sailing. I may have said that before but it is worth repeating. I compare this to when I make what others might regard as a mistake. I *never* make a mistake (I can hear your sharp in-drawing of breath, but calm down) - I have a *learning experience*. Now doesn't that sound so much better?

Since this homeopathy I was hearing so much about seemed to be completely safe I would give it a try. I found, almost on my doorstep, a medical doctor who was also qualified in and practised homeopathy. I believed this to be one of the universe's meaningful signs and made an appointment to see him. A few visits to this doctor set me off on another journey of discovery and I knew I had found a safe and natural treatment for some health issues. Perhaps I should say here that if I broke a leg my first call would be to a medical doctor! I'm not daft. But I almost certainly would go home and take the recommended homeopathic remedy for healing broken bones.

So what is homeopathy? What I found from my studies and I am still learning, is that the concept of "like cures like" was developed by Dr Samuel Hahnemann, a somewhat disillusioned German medical doctor who felt there had to be another way to treat illness. Dr Hahnemann lived in the eighteenth century and if you read of some of the treatments used at that time I'm not at all surprised   that he became disillusioned. The basic principle of like curing like though goes back way before Hahnemann's time, as it was known of during the life of Hippocrates. This term like cures like put simply means, if a substance in large doses produces a certain set of symptoms, that same substance in minute doses will alleviate or cure them. Homeopathy is more about symptoms than named illnesses, and as with so many other alternative therapies it treats the *whole* person. A homeopathic doctor will enquire into your way of life, mental and emotional states as well as your physical symptoms. Now doesn't that sound good! This method of treatment was definitely for me. Hahnemann also believed that less was more when it came to dosage. He set about finding out just how little of any substance worked. It's very hard to believe just how little that can be and the more diluted it is the more effective. Not only is a homeopathic remedy taken in the least possible dose but it is also taken for the least possible time. This was all sounding better and better, but perhaps this would be as good a time as any for me to make it absolutely clear that I believe that allopathic medicine combined with the more natural less invasive avenues to healing, would be my ideal good health routine.

Homeopathy is what we call a vibrational medicine, as is healing, and there are many more. An excellent book on vibrational healing is by Richard Gerber M.D. called *Vibrational Medicine for the 21st Century*. However if any therapy I write of in this book appeals to you, you may even just "feel" that something will help you, please visit a properly qualified therapist for an initial consultation. I am assuming you will already have consulted a medical doctor. Now don't be daft about this.

This "find" of mine, i.e. homeopathy, was quickly followed by that of flower remedies. What excitement for me, another tool to add to my self-help kit. I love flowers and gardening and here I could learn something else about flowers that I didn't know of. While I lived at home on the croft I was well accustomed to my mother picking leaves or flowers from "wild" plants or digging up their roots to make what I always referred to as "Mum's concoctions". These she used for the animals and very effective they were too. She always said it was a case of "needs must" as vets' visits were expensive and they would only be called to deal with serious problems. With an upbringing like this you can understand why I have this affinity with the witches of the past for most of them were no different to today's herbalists. Now I know homeopathy and flower remedies are quite different to herbal remedies but I am merely illustrating how my background from childhood of turning to nature for help, led to my ready acceptance of other natural ways of helping ourselves.

As with homeopathy, flower remedies are another vibrational medicine but it was again how these remedies were made that held my fascination. I only have experience of the Dr Bach remedies as they were all that were available to me at the time but there are now very many others. I am sure they are all equally beneficial but let me tell you a tiny bit about this

125

wonderful doctor who pioneered this therapy back in the early 1930's, around the time I was born.

As with Dr Hahnemann, Dr Bach also had a distinguished career in medicine but made time to research his own beliefs. These were that disease was found when there was disharmony between the spiritual and mental aspects of a human being. So the difference between the flower remedies and herbal preparations is that Dr Bach's flower remedies treat a person's state of mind, and this in turn he believed would heal the physical body.

Initially Dr Bach used the flower heads of a plant (other parts were sometimes used too), and these were floated on water and left in the sun for a few hours. This allowed the energy of the flower to be absorbed into the water. Yes, that *is* what I said. The flowers were then discarded and the water diluted many times. (This is very similar to the homeopathic "less is more" belief.) When bottled, this water had a tiny bit of brandy added to it to keep it fresh. Now grape juice is mostly used but I preferred the brandy! The dosage is a few drops in a glass of water or on the tongue, but in reality these drops are so safe they can be added to just about anything. They can be taken as often as you wish but please follow the instructions on the bottle. More than one remedy can be taken at a time but try to stick to no more than six. There is also a wonderful "Rescue Remedy" for emergencies. This comprises five remedies already mixed and my "Rescue" bottle lives in my bag at all times. Yes I am serious, these remedies are that good.

I very soon became quite experienced in diagnosing and making up bottles for people. As this is a very safe treatment we are dealing with here, I was allowed to do this under my healing insurance, but I was not allowed to charge any money for them. I could though accept a small donation to cover the cost of the glass bottle. The Bach Centre at that time had free leaflets on their remedies and on request they would send me liberal supplies of these. I made good use of them, giving them to anyone I could persuade to look closely at themselves and their life and then make their own choice of essences. Of course I supervised them when asked, but this encouraged people to take more control over their own health in a very safe and totally harmless way and it all worked beautifully.

One instance of using the Bach Remedies that comes readily to mind for me was of a lovely young boy (I'll call him Billy) who came for healing, with an adult of course. His problem was eventually diagnosed as a severe allergy to certain food colourings and other things as well. This can be quickly recognised now, but not so back then. The diagnosis in Billy's case took some time hence the visits to me, and as well as healing, I made him up a bottle of flower remedies for emergencies. He carried it with him at all times and called it Betty's Bottle. I was told that it was a godsend to him and it helped control some of his worst symptoms. This was an instance where healing and the flower remedies could support, but of course only the removal of the allergic substances finally returned Billy to normal health. I felt very privileged to be a support for this boy. I can hear the word placebo being whispered here. Of course I know this is not a placebo but even if it were, what is wrong with a placebo? Could other explanations for placebo perhaps be positive thinking, or belief? Surely we are simply back to the "we get what we expect" or "we can if we think we can" stuff. As a healer I don't care why or how a person gets well. The only thing that matters is that they do and that they stay that way.

So after having a wee word with your doctor you will find these remedies in every chemist's shop and others as well. Sometimes a small Bach book is available to purchase from the shops stocking the remedies. Failing that you will have to pay a visit to the appropriate section in your favourite bookshop. I promise you, you won't regret it.

To complete this chapter I will test your credulity even further. I would like to tell you about another discovery I made a little later and this time it was muscle testing. Although I was finding homeopathy of great benefit I still had some way to go and of course flower remedies treat the state of mind rather than direct physical problems. My "find" this time was something relatively new. This was muscle testing for allergies and intolerances. Again I found a medical doctor, not only trained in homeopathy but also in muscle testing specifically for allergies and intolerances. I had every confidence in this lady.

I was not disappointed as within one week of consulting her I was about 80% well. It transpired that my biggest problem was having North Sea gas brought into our home. Up until then gas was something my system had never had to cope with. To have any chance of wellness our two gas fires had to go immediately, but fortunately the central heating part of the system was tucked away where it wouldn't bother me.

Most of my household cleaning products had to go, and a host of other things we feel we need. This was when I had to make decisions about the problem of the formaldehyde that was in all the foam I depended on for my flower arranging business and the weekly classes I was teaching on this subject. When all this had to go it was very hard for me to bear. I also now had very little left in the way of an income. As I said earlier I solved part of that problem by changing over to teaching other subjects. I had given up roaming the countryside teaching crafts some time before this. I had done 32 years of that and felt it was time to move on.

As well as income from my new classes, and I loved the challenge of these, I reluctantly came to the conclusion that since healing was taking up so much of my time I would have to make a charge rather than rely on donations. Most of my people really welcomed this change and I learned to accept the odd few who considered that I should not be charging for my "gift from God" as I was sometimes told. I so wanted to reply to these people that it was a pity God couldn't see his way to sending me some supermarket vouchers for groceries. Instead I patiently explained that because I was spending so much time healing I could not be earning a living in other ways. It was therefore my time I was charging for.

By now you will be wondering what this muscle testing actually is and before you get the wrong idea, it has nothing to do with me going to a gym or anything daft like that. If I feel I need exercise I am much more likely to go plant a tree in my garden or mix some concrete and lay a few more slabs. Although I boast a little about still mixing concrete as a female octogenarian I will come clean about this. The truth is, I buy the cement stuff already mixed, no heavy shovelling for me, then I add water to small quantities of this mixture in an old basin or pail, and there I have a concrete mix. I should admit too that I'm not very good at it. My concrete mixes rarely stand the test of time. There now, my conscience is clear and I can return to the subject of muscle testing.

This therapy is based on our body's ability to let us know when a food, any substance, negative situations, *or even negative statements*, are likely to affect us in a detrimental way. Around the 1960's Dr John Goodheart found that muscles react immediately by going weak to any substance harmful to that person. On the other hand muscles stay strong when presented with any substance beneficial to that person. Now how weird is that then, we could ask. As with so many other bits of knowledge this had been known about for a long time before that, but it took Dr Goodheart to recognise what a "find" this was. A decade later he then made the surprising discovery that our muscles react to even emotional and intellectual stimuli.

Now this muscle testing was how my second homeopathic doctor identified all the things that my body was sensitive to. I know this can also be done by the medical profession in other ways but at that time this, I was told, was not an avenue open to me. Now I am only touching very lightly upon this subject because although I have done some training in it, not nearly enough to write authoritatively on the subject. But what I can tell you will be enough to stimulate your interest. On my first visit to my homeopathic doctor, I lay on a couch and relaxed. I raised my arm level with my shoulder, thumb pointing down and she asked me to resist any pressure she would put on my wrist using only two fingers to push my arm down. Placed on my solar plexus one at a time, were little twists of clingfilm and these contained tiny quantities of foods that I ate regularly. (We are unlikely to be allergic to anything that we only consume occasionally.) If this food was safe for me to have, my arm was easily strong enough to resist the pressure. If the food was likely to be harmful to me in any way my arm would immediately go weak even under only gentle pressure. Now how safe is that for a method of diagnosis? I never had any doubt that this lady would get me on the road to wellness, and muscle testing, in one form or another, has been my ally ever since. After all the food testing was completed this doctor then moved on to liquids which she had in tiny vials and the same with chemicals. (Now all foods can be tested in vials.) As I have said it was when we reached this stage that the true origins of my problems showed up. Of course as well as ridding my home and diet of as many allergens as possible I also had homeopathic treatment.

So now along with the other therapies I had studied, I was able to point people gently in the direction of muscle testing whenever I felt that this was advisable. This form of testing of course requires two people, a patient and a tester, and this, for any serious problem is still by far the safest and most reliable way forward. However I later learned of other methods of testing and these don't necessarily require a second person. My original homeopath has retired but I have a very good friend who is also well qualified in muscle testing, and with her help I have made other discoveries about myself. My friend's approach to treatment differs slightly in that she spends time exploring the possible reasons why any allergies have developed in the first place. As I am sure you will all know, finding and if possible removing the cause is the real solution to any problem.

CHAPTER 12

MY WONDERFUL WORLD OF

COLOUR

A few miles away from where I live a healing and retreat centre opened. What an exciting happening that was. Now I had access to an unbelievable amount of information from courses and almost as important, sharing with other like-minded people. There were one, two and three day courses on such things as astrology, art therapy, stones, sound therapy, colour and so many more. We had visits from Indian mystics, I didn't take to them much and we had mediums. They were usually excellent and I was quite a good judge of mediumship by then.

Two evenings a month I led a meditation and healing session there. As I was a full healer member of the NFSH I was allowed to sponsor probationers (now called students), and these evenings, with the public invited along to participate, were my students' experience opportunities. When starting healing development, practising on family and friends is good for a time, but so much more experience can be gained from working with complete strangers. I would lead a visualisation at the start of the evening and then allocate people to students for healing. Some evenings I might only have three or four students but twenty plus people. Then I would seat the healers back to back in the middle of a circle and we would do a group distant healing exercise, even though the distance between healers and people was minimal. Once I sensed the healing energy flowing freely between all of us, I would get those receiving the energy to join hands, and then ask them to concentrate on circulating that energy round the group. This exercise was always a huge success and from these small beginnings more and more people were introduced to channelling the healing energy themselves. This was a very fulfilling and even busier time for me.

Going back a little in time, one of the courses that came to the centre near me was a colour therapy training course, run by a lady called Marie Louise Lacy. I had seen the advertisement for it and decided that this was definitely meant for me. By now it seemed that everything I touched or took up as a hobby turned into something I either taught or earned a little money from. My gardening had turned into my dried flower arranging business. My interest in crafts and embroidery had turned into teaching these subjects. As I explain later even my healing turned into tutoring on behalf of the NFSH. But this colour course would be for me and me alone. It was perhaps selfish of me but I had made up my mind that I would not get involved in doing any of the talks or teaching as I had with my other interests. Indeed I never even expected to be good enough to gain a diploma. The training was over two years and then if we passed that part we could work towards a diploma. I must have been the first to enrol. Some time before this, quite by chance, I had stumbled upon this lady's book *Know Yourself through Colour*, now out of print, and I *knew* I had to buy it. I couldn't then believe my good fortune in being given the opportunity to do Marie Louise's colour course and only a few miles away too. I knew that she had spent time tutoring in America, and back then I would never have guessed that some years on I would follow in her footsteps and do the same. It would be understandable to think that this is a strange world of coincidences, but then we must all know by now that in this totally ordered universe there is no such thing as a coincidence.

One strange happening I feel I would like to mention was that for a week to ten days before each course, every time I went into a room and was faced with a white wall or surface, there would appear the most wonderful splodges of colour on that surface. "Splodges" described them perfectly for they had no shape and although most of them were violet I did see other colours as well. Then too as I drove down a street

I would notice the double yellow lines next to the pavement, but beside those lines very clearly would be another set in the colour violet. Of course in this case I was seeing the colour and the complementary. I still occasionally see this today. Seeing the lines bit is easily explained and I later used a version of this as a teaching exercise, but I can only imagine that the splodges of colour on, usually my bathroom door were the result of my total focus on colour at that time and it showed just how important this was to become in my life. Later I was given another possible explanation and I explain about this in another chapter. This was very definitely believe or not stuff.

Just in case this may be of interest to anyone I will give a brief explanation of colours and complementaries. A colour therapist may work with a colour wheel that varies slightly from that used by artists because of the inclusion of the colour magenta. When this wheel is used the complementary colours vary a little from those generally accepted as such. However there is a very easy and interesting way of finding the true complementary to any colour. This is by using our eyes,. If we look for a few seconds at any colour, then immediately shift our gaze to a pure white surface, the colour that comes up on that surface will be the true complementary to the original colour looked at. Now I do appreciate that this bit of information may not be of huge use to you in your daily lives, but my head is full of stuff like this and I like to share!

Getting back to my colour course, could I have been happier with so many new things to learn? I don't think so. Just before I was due to sit my diploma exam (yes I did get there, how could I not?) Marie Louise approached me and asked if I would take over tutoring her training courses in Scotland. Her school was also called *Know Yourself through Colour*. As she was spending so much time in America she was appointing tutors in Scotland, England and Northern Ireland. I remember putting forward half a dozen reasons why I would not be a suitable candidate for this position. I was very good at self-sabotage then, due of course to a fear of not being good enough. Marie Louise listened to none of them.

When I told my family (who by this time had heard nothing but colour from me for many months) they laughingly discussed, not *whether* I would take up this challenge, but how long it would take me to accept. Marie Louise had given me a month to decide. After I got over the not being good enough bit, I made up my mind in less than a week. And so I set off on another of life's journeys. I have already explained that I viewed my education in all this spiritual stuff like putting together a huge jigsaw puzzle. Piece after piece fell into place adding more and more to my understanding of the Universe and man's part in it. Marie Louise filled in quite a significant part of this jigsaw in those two years and opened my mind to so much more. My jigsaw is still a long way from completion and I can't fully express the wonder and pleasure each time another piece falls into place. They are truly "Aha" moments for me.

Some of the subjects included on the colour course I have covered in separate chapters, because Marie Louise's teaching inspired me to delve deeper into them. A few others I would like to share here. Early on we were taught how to work out a person's strengths and weaknesses from knowing their favourite colour. This choice would also reveal their likes, dislikes, possible careers to follow and much more, and in many talks to different audiences over the years I have found this to be over 80% accurate. That's pretty high for general audiences with no opportunity for one to one discussion. Of course our colour preferences change a few times over our lifetime because *we* change as we learn more and develop different aspects of our character. The whole purpose of a life on earth is to progress towards perfection. That is why one lifetime here can never be enough. I dread to think how many more lives on this earth I'm going to need.

The psychology of colour was and still is my greatest love where colour is concerned. Counselling was the follow on subject to this and art therapy for a little light relief was also included. Practising on each other in class was great fun but it was a little scary later on to work with strangers. I have always preferred teaching and speaking on colour to giving private consultations, although of course I had to be prepared to do these too, particularly when I was in America.

On one course we were led through a lecture on the Platonic Solids and I am ashamed to say that Plato and I did not get on well. First I discovered that he hadn't discovered these shapes at all. They were known of quite a while before he took an interest in them, although he did name them after himself. A bit underhand I thought. I eventually managed to absorb enough of this subject to get me by, but not a lot more. For instance I do know that these shapes are said to be the building blocks of everything in our world including our bodies. After that this subject got a bit blurred for me. Perhaps I wasn't alone in this because I got the distinct feeling that this wasn't Marie Louise's favourite subject either. Some time later when I was teaching this subject and M.L. was sitting in on my lecture and assessing my competence, she congratulated me on my understanding of this subject. If only she had known that I had been burning the midnight oil just beforehand, in order to get enough of the subject to sink in, to enable me to do my lecture on it. I prayed for few questions that day and my luck held. I think this might be called "winging it". This was the only subject that I ever found dodgy to teach. The subject wasn't dodgy of course, only my knowledge of it. I was able though to show my students my beautiful set of tiny amethyst quartz crystal Platonic Solid shapes, and because I had a blind student in my class at that time I had also made very large cardboard shapes of each one so that this student could handle them and get a better idea of what I was talking about. Making these shapes actually taught me more about them than any lecture could. Just in case it is of interest, the shapes are –

Hexahedron – said to be green and associated with the earth and our sense of smell

Octahedron – yellow – air - sound

Tetrahedron – red – fire - sight

Icosahedron – blue – water - taste

Dodecahedron – violet – ether - touch

and now we can see the relation to colour and why this was included in my colour training and teaching.

Now if Plato didn't excite me, Pythagoras and his numbers certainly did. Here was a man I would have loved to meet. Perhaps I wouldn't have been too keen to have lived in his time in history and goodness knows what he would have made of my world today. When I learned that number one vibrates with the colour red, number two with orange and so on until we come to numbers eight and nine and they are said to vibrate with silver and gold, then numerology made perfect sense to me and another jigsaw piece fell into place. Numerology works mostly on our date of birth and adding those numbers together until we have a single digit. When I did this for my own birth date I just couldn't believe how accurate numerology could be. I don't use numerology every day. My life isn't like that, mostly I just get on with it without checking out this or that to see if I am on the right path, but I do love to draw up a chart for a new baby. Good books abound here too and don't be too surprised if you too fall under its spell. I'm sure though, if any of the things I have written about had been introduced to me in isolation, I would have been inclined to dismiss most of them out of hand. It was the gradual introduction to one thing after another with the connections between them being thoroughly explained and understood that led to my acceptance of so much.

There were many other subjects covered on M.L.'s course where I could immediately see the connection with colour. For instance – take a little look at essential oils. Oils derived from the different coloured flowers tied in with our other colour information. Oils derived from red, orange and yellow flowers are stimulating in different ways, just as the colours are, green is the balancer in the middle and oils from blue, deeper blue/indigo and violet flowers are calming. This explains why lavender oil helps us sleep and so on. Now that was all easy for me to understand. As you will have guessed this is a much simplified explanation of the relation of colour to essential oils.

We learned too of the influence colour has in advertising. That opened our eyes a bit. M.L. of course, as I said earlier, had been involved as a consultant in this at one point and this helped to make this lecture even more interesting and revealing. I rarely even look at ads on television any more. Not only will the main colours in any ad influence us but even the background colours are carefully chosen to persuade us to buy. Briefly if a manufacturer wants to sell a very expensive and very fast sports car, using relaxing colours is hardly going to attract the type of person who buys a sports car is it? And what colour would be used to promote something natural, safe and harmless to the environment? Why green, of course, what else? Something fresh and clean? Very often lemon/ yellow. I could go on and on but you will all have noticed these connections for yourself. When you read the chapter on sound you will be able to connect the music used in ads too. Using colour in the home was another favourite subject of mine and this could fill a book on its own. Indeed Marie Louise has a book *"The Power of Colour to heal the Environment"* covering not only colour in our homes but which colours would be appropriate for use in many other buildings too. I heed this aspect of colour totally, as I do with which colours to wear. I simply will not wear any colours that I do not feel right for me on any particular day and this usually depends on what I am going to be doing that day. To understand this better, take a look at the colours mostly worn by sportsmen and sportswomen. The colours that give us energy usually abound here. Briefly red gives us energy, orange helps us with our creativity, yellow – our thinking, green – to be laid back about things, sometimes too much so, blue – communication, violet – connecting with higher energy frequencies and magenta – wow!

I had a private consultation with M.L. early on and I was amazed at just how much she could tell me about myself from my choice of three colours. She used colour cards for this. She was also a wonderful medium, but not in the sense of contacting dead relatives, I never once heard her do that, but in being able to channel a much deeper wisdom than I felt I ever could. She had also had the great privilege of having met some very wise people indeed from many other parts of the world. One of these was Omraam Mikael Aivanhov and M.L. spent a great deal of time over the years listening and learning from his lectures at his home in France. He was Bulgarian by birth. Much of what he had taught her she incorporated into the courses. I have most of Aivanhov's lectures as these were subsequently printed in book form.

Now I have given you enough about my training in colour. As I said much of the rest features in other chapters. I taught on behalf of Marie Louise for a few years until my life fell apart when my husband Frank died. After nursing him for a lengthy period I was physically, mentally and emotionally drained and I really did need to find a purpose to go on living. I was still only 65 and I had to find a way through the darkness and into the light again. I knew Frank expected this of me and I couldn't let him down. He remains close.

My daughter had qualified in colour therapy too by this time and we discussed starting our own training school together. We were sitting in my summerhouse and were at the "will we/won't we" stage when a white feather floated down past the open doors to land in front of us. I took this as a positive sign and that was the birth of "Through the Spectrum" our very own training course. Because of my association with Marie Louise I was accepted and accredited by the then governing body the International Association of Colour and also by the Institute of Complementary Medicine. We were off the two of us and flying high.

145

CHAPTER 13

I didn't like the SOUND of this much!

While doing my colour training Marie Louise told us one day that the next subject we would be studying would be "Sound". My heart sank, for little did *she* know how little *I* knew of this subject. Of course my mind turned immediately to music when the word sound was mentioned. That really just confirmed how little I knew of how wide ranging a subject this would be. I had been told at an early age that I was "tone deaf". I had no idea what this meant. However it wasn't hard to get the message that I wasn't considered to be of musical bent. Of course this might have been comparative! Before the start of the Second World War one of my brothers Teddy played the chanter with big ideas about graduating to the bagpipes. We found it hard to stand the sound of a piper who still needed "L" plates. I swear when Teddy was practising the "pipes" our whole house vibrated. The dog cowered in a shed out the back and I would feel a great need to go and play with the boy next door. Dad would go and dig the furthest corner of the garden and Mum would go the few hundred yards up the road to the well for water. Such was the power of the skirl of the bagpipes. To be fair to my brother he was very good on other instruments and he did get better on the pipes.

Another brother, Sandy, played both the piano accordion and the button keyed accordion. He was very good too. Of course they were both self-taught and neither could read music. Every piece of music they played was picked up by listening to it and taking the tune from there. Surely that has to be a skill in itself. Another brother Alfie had the most beautiful tenor voice and was very well known as a singer, both locally and further afield too. By the time I joined the family my Dad didn't sing very much but he also had an excellent voice. I will never forget the winter evenings of music and song dirling out from our home. Of course tone deaf or not I refused to be left out and was usually given a comb and a piece of thin paper and succeeded in making sounds of a sort by wrapping the paper round the teeth of the comb, putting it to my lips and blowing through it. This hardly contributed anything to the music but hopefully didn't detract too much from it either. Most of my family too could yodel (our dog loved that and joined in) but I haven't heard a yodeller in a long time, not even when I visited Switzerland. I remember in the films of the time cowboys could almost all yodel. Another instrument in the house was the harmonica or mouthie. It wasn't very highly rated as an instrument as it was considered that anyone could get a tune out of the mouthie. Except me of course. So what chance had I of being recognised as musical? Lastly we always had a little melodeon lying around as this was my Dad's area of expertise along with the jew's-harp. I really feel, due to my total lack of musical ability that I let our side down rather badly, and here I was expected to study sound, or music as I mistakenly thought.

Marie Louise was unaware of the stony ground she was about to till. I quickly found though that this subject, as with all the others, fascinated me, and again I was "in my element". Perhaps I'm not so tone deaf after all for I immediately found that I could "feel" sound. Marie Louise's teaching was all about how music in different keys affected our bodies. I had no trouble in sensing which parts of my body were being affected by different pieces of music. Another piece of my jigsaw slipped into place.

According to what I was taught then and much reading since, and yes of course I needed more books, l learned that music played in different keynotes has a distinct effect on our body. Marching compositions arranged in the key of "C" will energise our body from the thighs down, and we may even feel our feet tapping in time to the music. When we feel a bit "high" this is the music to listen to – it will bring us back down to earth very quickly. The instruments too play their part. Drums come readily to mind for the key of "C" and since this key vibrates at 256Hz as does the colour red we begin to understand why, in the past, drums were the chosen instrument to lead armies into battle. Red is a colour well known as an energiser and a giver of courage, hence its use in uniforms and standards.

Staying just a little longer in the context of battles, I read recently that after a conflict had commenced there was little left for the drummer boys to do, until it was discovered by chance that using their drumsticks to tap rhythmically on injured limbs greatly reduced pain. This discovery I understand is the forerunner to many pulsating pain relief instruments in use today. Obviously I can't vouch for the truth of this but it sounds probable and ideas always come from somewhere. Can you understand why I get so carried away by all this stuff?

Back to our keynotes. Music in the key of "D" will vibrate with the sacral centre, and a spin off here is improved creativity amongst other benefits. My husband was a keen painter and always played music while he painted, but I was never sure which made him more creative, the music or the large glass of wine by his hand. In the key of "E" our solar plexus area will benefit, calming our nervous system. Up now to around the heart and the key of "F", romantic music is frequently in this key, so the connection here is obvious. It shares a vibration just about 340Hz with the colour green. A great deal of music with the word green in the title is in the key of "F". Or so I am told as you will appreciate I wouldn't know.

The remaining keys affecting our physical body are "G" around the throat, then "A" the brow, relating to our intuition, thoughts etc. and finally "B" the crown of the head connecting us to higher realms or God if you prefer. Music in this key is excellent for meditation and will take us soaring high. Follow this with a burst of one of Suza's Marches and we come back down to earth with a bump. Not to be recommended incidentally – it gives one a headache. I know. I've done it! One must come back down to earth very slowly after meditation.

On this course too we even studied the work of some of the great composers of the past, and how their music affected the whole world at that time. Of course since their music is still being played it must have the same effect today. Initially I found it very hard to get my mind round this, but I had to acknowledge that as I was physically feeling the effect of sound in the different parts of my own body, why shouldn't we collectively be influenced by some of these great works? Can you see how far all this took me along this road in my quest for knowledge and understanding? And how many more bits of my jigsaw fell into place? The only drawback to all this learning was and still is, that the more I learn the more I realise just how little I know! But then that is life.

I had another learning experience while I was in Chicago. I had the opportunity to listen and play with crystal bowls. Yes, bowls actually made from quartz crystal. The largest at that time was 18" in diameter and others went down to 5". These my hostess tapped very softly with a little rubber mallet, and sometimes she sounded them by rubbing the mallet very gently round the rim of the bowl until a resonance was built up. This was exactly as we can do with crystal glasses. The sound of the bowls was just wonderful and since they are each said to resonate with a different keynote, again I could feel the sound in the different parts of my body. Now I do not have the knowledge or experience to give more details about these bowls, (they were far too expensive for me to buy) but in the hands of a skilled and experienced healer they can be used to balance the body through the energy centres, by matching the correct bowl to each of the centres. At one time I would have considered using quartz crystal bowls for healing very weird indeed, and yet there I was in America, a country I never wanted to visit, not only accepting that this was possible, but actually using and loving them.

Marie-Louise also introduced me briefly to tuning forks. I certainly remembered in music classes at school seeing the teacher using a tiny tuning fork when we were about to start a singing lesson. Totally wasted on me of course, but nevertheless this little piece of metal fascinated me and for some reason I always wanted to own one. But these were not the tuning forks Marie-Louise was lecturing on. The ones she had were called Pythagorean forks and I later came to own a whole set of these and I prize them highly. I tell of how I acquired them in the chapter about my trip to Chicago. These are used for healing in exactly the same way as the crystal bowls, by matching the correct fork to the relevant energy centre. After an initial consultation a healer would either sound the matching tuning fork over the relevant energy centre to balance it, or alternatively a whole body treatment might be preferred sounding each of the forks in turn over all the major energy centres of the body. A whole treatment is a lovely experience and the vibrations from each tuning fork can be easily felt, particularly those relating to the areas from the waist down. Because I was unable to get any further training in this method of healing in Scotland at that time, I kept my tuning forks for practising with friends and self-treating. I would prefer a medical doctor though if I suspected I had broken a bone somewhere or had appendicitis. But tuning forks would certainly be good if used to aid my recovery as would my homeopathy and various other therapies.

Our tutor covered many other aspects of sound such as the use of the voice in meditation and mantras, she showed us bells, balls and bowls in different metals and we got a good grounding in their uses. All of these were beautiful things to have and hold and I do own one or two just for this reason. The next two bits of information certainly weren't part of our colour training but they do fit into the believe it or not category and so I'm sure you will find them of interest. I am including them in the Sound chapter because in both cases they involve the use of the voice. The first is to do with plants, to be more precise, talking to them. This is something I have done for years and I know I am in good company. However it was only a few years ago that I was shown proof that my plants are capable of hearing me and reacting to my voice.

On one of my trips to London I thoroughly enjoyed and was greatly impressed by a speaker called Cleve Backster. He had only a few copies of his book with him called *Primary Perception* and I was lucky enough to secure a copy by slipping out smartly just before the lunch break. The opportunity to have a book written by someone else who talked to plants just could not be missed.

Cleve started off by giving us a bit of his background. His story gets interesting when he reaches the point where he is working with polygraph machines. These he was using as lie detectors. In humans they measure and record the pulse rate and strength, the respiration and any change in blood pressure, hence their importance as lie detectors. One particular morning while watering his dracaena plant in

153

his lab he had the idea of connecting this machine to one of this plant's large leaves. He wanted to test whether the polygraph machine would perchance measure the uptake of water from root to leaf of this plant. He explained all this in detail but I relate it briefly as I had not taken any notes at the lecture. The result of this experiment was the opposite of what he expected, as the machine showed a similar reaction by the plant to that of a human in fear of detection or when feeling threatened! He then tried dipping one of its leaves in his hot cup of coffee. The polygraph registered a similar reaction from the plant to that of a person when bored! Cleve had to think again. He then came up with the thought, note - it was thought only at this point, that he would light a match and burn the leaf attached to the polygraph. He was standing some fifteen feet from the plant and a few feet from the machine. He was alone in the lab and nothing had changed in the room apart from his thinking. The plant's instant dramatic reaction was recorded by the pen of the polygraph. Cleve then left the room to fetch some matches. When he returned the reading was still the same. On changing his mind and removing the matches from the room the reading all settled down. Later a colleague entered the room and made a threatening remark to this plant, and there was another dramatic reaction from the plant!

The happening that day was the start of Backster's research into biocommunication and this went on for years. The remainder of his lecture was just as interesting, if not more so. His book makes fascinating reading and once again opens one's mind to this wonderful world around us and to just how little we truly know of it. Of course I continue to talk to my plants and I know now that they can hear me so I am very careful what I say!

The other story is equally mind boggling but I have not had the privilege of meeting this researcher, nor have I heard him speak, but I still feel I want to tell you of his research into freezing water. Now what is so unusual about that you may ask? Read on. This man's name is Masaru Emoto and he is Japanese. His research as I have just said has been with water, and the effect spoken words (this is the sound connection again) and printed words have on water. He found that when water is spoken to lovingly using positive words only and then this water is frozen, beautiful crystal patterns are made. This applies too when positive and kind printed words are shown to water or attached to the dish containing the water, they produce equally beautiful crystal patterns. The opposite effect is found when negative or harsh words are used. Masaru Emoto's research proves that the energy of words whether spoken or printed transmits to water and since our bodies are 70% water what effects are negative words having on us? I have always believed that they have a profound effect and should be used kindly at all times. And what of our thoughts? Well surely Cleve Backster's research proves that even our thoughts have more effect on the world around us than we can possible imagine.

I remember way back when I was first being introduced to so many new concepts, I was told repeatedly of how our thoughts and words affected everyone around us and how careful we must all be to make them positive and kind. I did find this idea hard to believe but I didn't dismiss it. I just kept an open mind as with so many other things I was learning at the time. Now between Cleve Backster's research and that of Masaru Emoto, and both are very extensive, I have no hesitation whatsoever in adding another piece to my jigsaw. Emoto's books, of which there are several, have many photographs of his beautiful and of his distorted water crystals, and after all this is not so different to the effect of sound on sand when it too forms beautiful patterns.

Now how is that for another whole lot of believe or not stuff?

CHAPTER 14

CHICAGO – HERE I COME!

Quite out of the blue one day I had a phone call from a friend asking me if I would like to teach my colour courses in America – Chicago to be precise. She had a friend from there staying with her at that time, and this friend was opening a new healing centre on the outskirts of Chicago. I was now being asked to run the first training courses handselling this centre. What a shock that was to my system. Ever since I seriously started healing and committing myself to it, I had repeatedly told God I would do anything to further healing but I wasn't going to travel very far to anywhere. Admittedly the chances of that happening were slim indeed. Or so I thought. My ears didn't do planes you see and for some reason I had never had any desire to go to America. There were other reasons for me not wanting to go far afield and they all boiled down to lack of confidence in myself, and I also had to admit I was terrified at the very thought of travelling abroad. I am very much a home bird, and so my reply to my friend was a loud and clear, "No thank you". I had already squirmed out of accepting an invitation to speak on colour therapy in Poland and I felt I had a narrow escape getting out of that one, so I was taking no chances with this American business. I admit I had managed to travel as far as Glasgow on one occasion to speak to a large group of healers on the subject of colour. I can hear you thinking "big deal", so perhaps a little more of an explanation is necessary. Up until my husband died I would travel anywhere as long as he was with me. Sometimes not too willingly, as in our visits to France, but I would do it for him. Left on my own this was one thing I found it difficult to find the courage to tackle. I offer no mitigating excuses. I am just a travelling wimp.

Now it happened that I was going to a talk the following evening and this American lady was to be the speaker. I don't know now how it came about, but I arrived back home very late that night committed to this American trip. At least I had the good sense to restrict my teaching commitment to colour psychology only. This aspect of colour was and still is my great love, and it meant having to take a lot less "stuff" with me in the way of colour therapy teaching aids. I would have to dye around a hundred large silk squares in all the colours of the rainbow though, but they would be easy to transport. These would be for my students' use. I suppose all I can say in defence of this radical change of mind was that I firmly believe, as I have already said, that we are all here having this earthly life in order to learn and meeting challenges is a very good way of doing that. Now I had already dodged Poland so I realised that perhaps it would be tempting fate to dodge America too. There might just be something even bigger thrown my way. My friend God has a habit of doing that to me. And after all, perhaps I might just enjoy America, I thought.

The day of my flight, America declared war on Iraq. Great start. On arrival at O'Hare airport just outside Chicago the atmosphere was very tense. I could sense fear all around me. There were policemen and security men everywhere, all carrying guns. Now this may have been common practice for them, but their attitude to the public that day was quite alien to me and I found this really scary. Unfortunately my luggage was lost and I had to report this causing complications. At the nearest point allowed, my hostess met me, and warned me very firmly to do exactly as I was told until I was clear of the building. No cheeky or over friendly remarks she warned. The security people were apparently in an "arresting" mood. I was treated reasonably well, but it was not so for anyone of Middle Eastern appearance. I found it hard to stand by and watch when I saw one such family with three very small excited children being dealt with quite roughly. It was made abundantly clear to me even, that when I was told to stand on a small spot on the floor, I must not move one inch from that spot. What chance had anyone with small children? I was beginning to think that perhaps the Poland job might have been a better bet after all. I did eventually escape after being given an emergency allowance to buy some necessary items. Not the best start to my trip though. I had been a bag of nerves before leaving, the flight was long and tiring and then I arrived to find men with guns, bullying of little ones, and to cap it all I had no clean underwear. I could have been forgiven for thinking that God was being a little less than supportive.

My hosts for the trip had quite a large house, well very large really. For instance the clothes closet in my bedroom was about the same size as my small bedroom at home and I had never actually seen a television set as big as this one was, not even in a shop window, and in the corner of the screen was a large red "high alert" sign. It never altered all the time I was there. No wonder everyone I met was in such an extreme state of alarm and could not believe I had actually chosen to travel on a plane at that time. Of course the Twin Towers attack was still very fresh in their memory and indeed I was told that we would not be able to go anywhere near the Sears Tower on my visit, as they seriously expected it to be the next target. I tried not to be too overwhelmed by my surroundings, nor the atmosphere, but considering my quiet background I found everything was just SO BIG. I don't "do" big very comfortably. I found it strange too that they hung out an American flag every day on the house front and took it in at night. This was a mark of respect apparently and forgetting to take this flag in at night was an actual offence. The only flag hanging I had ever known (apart from public buildings) was when my Dad borrowed a Union Jack, climbed up and attached it to the chimney of our croft house for my wedding day. At the time he joked that he was celebrating getting me off his hands, but I knew he liked me really!

After a few days in Chicago when the tension was easing a little, it was decided that it would be safe to visit their Museum. I wanted to see the textile collection, but here again I was a little unlucky. We had unwittingly chosen to go there at exactly the same time as the Dalai Lama – so more security and guns everywhere and huge parts of the building closed off to the public. I very nearly didn't get in at all, as I was carrying a small paper bag with a few slices of wheat free bread kindly given to me at the restaurant where we had lunch. This was indeed a strange world I was in, apparently a few slices of bread was a "suspicious package" and I had to give a satisfactory explanation for possessing it. (I had an intolerance to wheat at the time and this bread was manna from heaven for me. The security men were unimpressed with this explanation but eventually capitulated and let me pass.) At one point on this visit I did pass the time of day with the Dalai Lama's second in command. My hostess had recognised him as she had met him before on her travels. He must have considered me safe to converse with, despite my bread, but our conversation didn't amount to much really. I suppose I was a wee bit out of my comfort zone, but it was good to talk even briefly, with such a thoroughly nice man.

Prior to our arrival I had been booked in on a workshop making a North American Indian medicine pouch in leather with lots of bead decoration. This was the evening after I arrived and although I was very jetlagged I wasn't going to miss a moment of this experience. Making things is another great love of mine and Indian medicine bags aren't much seen in the North East of Scotland. Our teachers that evening were all pure Indian and such beautiful, kind people. To my surprise I felt completely at home with them. Had I been here too in a past life? Surely not, but I did feel good and making the little medicine bag was very easy for me and I still treasure it. Mind you I haven't found much use for it so far, but there's still time.

Another highlight of my visit was when I was asked to do "door duty" one morning, this for clients who were booked in with my hostess. I was more than happy to oblige, and particularly so when the first client introduced himself on arrival and turned out to be one of the American astronauts. Now how much more exciting could this trip get I wondered? Over and above all these new experiences I did actually teach colour classes in Chicago although attendance numbers were lower than I would have liked. There had been cancellations due no doubt to this ever present climate of fear gripping the country. I also did some private consultations on colour and met more lovely people. Some weeks after I returned home one of them made me a gift of a whole set of tuning forks used in sound therapy. These were the ones I mentioned earlier and they were something I simply could not have afforded to buy for myself and I was overwhelmed by this lady's generosity.

In between teaching and consultations I saw a little of the countryside surrounding Chicago too, and it all reminded me of when I was a child and sitting in the ninepenny seats at the picture house watching Westerns. Another thrill for me was seeing the long trucks and hearing the noise they made when passing by on the highway, they too rekindled memories. Perhaps I spent too much time at the pictures when I was young. I was curious too about the enormous water storage tanks dotting the landscape. They were not things of beauty but of necessity. Living in Scotland all my life I am accustomed to and take for granted our beautiful mountains, hills, lochs and rivers all naturally bringing our copious rainfall to lower levels. I was now visiting an almost flat plain and immediately understood the need for storage tanks.

However interesting though those experiences were, the biggest impact of my visit was a meditation evening run by hostess in her teaching studio in her home. I'm off back to the spooky believe it or not stuff again by the way. I was an honoured guest at this meditation and was expected to share my thoughts with the group at the end of the evening. I considered this quite a privilege, especially when I found that almost everyone present was of North American Indian descent and my background was so different to theirs – or was it? Although quite an accomplished meditator by this time, I did wonder how I was going to relax after all the exciting things I had been experiencing since my arrival in what I believed to be a country new to me – or, as I said, was it? Let me tell you of my first meditation experience in America.

The music chosen for the evening was well known to me. It was "Solitudes" by Dan Gibson recorded with nature sounds from the Algonquin Park in Canada. I had listened to this many times at home and used it regularly for meditation purposes with groups. It always had a profound effect on me and on others. I found it hauntingly beautiful, full of the sounds of running water, wolves and birds. Listening to it that evening in Chicago, to my surprise, in my mind, I was immediately transported back in time and saw an Indian settlement full of men and women, children playing with their dogs, and horses tethered loosely nearby. The scene was very peaceful and I knew that I was part of it as a young Indian squaw. These were my people. Here I was loved, cherished and happy. I could still hear the music and the other sounds in the background. They fitted completely into the picture I was now part of.

Gradually this peaceful scene faded and I was aware, again in my mind, of being with a group of white settlers some years forward in time. These too were my people, but now I was a young man and taking part in planning an attack on an Indian settlement. We needed to clear the Indians from their homes in order to farm the land and build a cattle ranch. Ruthlessly I took part in the killing. Blood ran everywhere, the blood of men, women and children. We took no prisoners and we allowed no one to escape. It was a complete massacre.

The music again filtered back into my mind and the reality of what I had just taken part in, hit me. I felt heavy with sorrow, guilt and shame. How could I have done it? So much slaughter. As the music softly faded out I found myself back in my normal state and aware once more of the group. I looked at these gentle wonderful people who had so kindly invited me into their lives and I wondered how I could share any of what I had experienced. Just then words dropped into my head from seemingly nowhere and I knew the message I was meant to share. "What we do unto others, we do unto ourselves". Profound words now indelibly impressed on my mind, and so apt for a week when, for their country, yet another conflict had just begun.

165

Had I really once had a life as a North American Indian and again as a settler in that part of the world? Certainly, for the whole of my stay there, I did feel that just for a time I had come home. Or could it have been that I was sensitive to and picking up the vibrational history of the area? The truth I will never know, in this life anyway.

One last interesting thing before I leave Chicago. Ever since my arrival, every morning around 6a.m. I listened to a train passing a short distance away, and on hearing its whistle I was once more transported back to the world of the Westerns at our local cinema in Stonehaven. The train would whistle once for a few seconds only, and I just loved the sound of it. Now during my stay, I had been out for dinner with my hosts and a few of their friends. Another of their guests was a local radio DJ and we had a long chat together about everything I had so enjoyed on my visit. I told him of the train whistle and how I had even started wakening early just to hear it. This DJ seemed quite taken with this story. Forward now to my very last night in Chicago when I had slept very little. I was by this time getting very anxious about the journey home. Then, just a little earlier than usual, I heard in the far distance "my" train whistle – on and on it sounded, as it got nearer and nearer, and on and on it went into the far distance. I could barely contain my excitement. Could this DJ have organised this farewell just for me? Somehow I think that was quite likely. Wherever that train driver is now – I thank him. He made my visit to his country complete.

P.S. I was told later that as we were on our way to the airport for my flight home, a phone call came through from Oprah Winfrey's office looking to discuss with me the possibility of a television interview. How was that for a narrow escape? That might just have been a challenge too far for me.

CHAPTER 15

MORE HEALING HISTORY

Because I get so carried away with all that I have learned over the years, and I have so wished to share as much of it as possible, I feel I may have neglected to keep you up to date with all that was happening in my spiritual or energy healing world. Healing has fallen away quite a bit in recent years and that is a great pity as it can be so beneficial and supportive in many ways. But then too, training in other therapies is now readily available, some encompassing energy healing, and things do tend to go in cycles. So who knows what the future may hold?

Back in the early days healing was perceived by some to be miraculous, and a few would be a bit disappointed when the miracle didn't always happen. An important point here too was the exact definition of a miracle to each person. This definition can be very relative. If someone had suffered great pain for months, any lessening of that pain was to them, a miracle. This definition would not be true for everyone. On seeing a person for the first time I would always ask what their expectations were from healing. This was very important to me in deciding how best I could help them. Sometimes it was necessary to point out, very gently of course, that I had not yet reached the level of walking on water! Yes on the odd occasion expectations were rather unrealistic, but then how could I fault this when I keep telling you that, "What we perceive we can achieve". The stumbling block here was that those who expected the most from healing, were the ones who were prepared to do the least to help themselves.

With most people too, I needed to know that they had seen their doctor, even to the point of giving initial healing but then explaining that I couldn't see them again until they *had* seen their G.P. At times too I felt I needed to inform their doctor of my findings when giving healing. This was in accordance with the Healing Trust's Code of Conduct, but of course this could be done only with the permission of the person concerned. On one occasion I was called to a lady late one evening. In this case her doctor had visited earlier and diagnosed flu. My "feeling" was that there was a problem in her brain. I knew no more than that. However I felt it was my responsibility to pass this on to her doctor with the lady's permission and without worrying her too much. This I did on my return home. Next day I had a call to say this lady had just died of a

169

brain haemorrhage. Now I was convinced that it was this person's time to go and nothing could have been done to save her, but I was very relieved that I had followed my instinct and the correct procedure.

One other such case I would tell you of. This person had experienced what I could only describe as being similar to an epileptic fit while in my healing room. I followed the correct First Aid procedure and supported her until she recovered. I had trained in First Aid when my children were little. Perhaps this was pre-empting a skill I would need for my future, but it is also covered in our healing training. Again, with this lady's permission, I reported to her doctor exactly what had happened in my home. He was polite, but cool and distant. Some hours later another doctor phoned me and asked me to repeat what I had already reported. The upshot of all this was that it was discovered that each new drug this person had been prescribed she added to those she was already taking, instead of replacing them. This mixture of drugs had led to the episode I witnessed and I was told that this could have been fatal. I was even more glad this time that I had followed our healing rules.

I tell of these two incidents to help you understand how huge was the responsibility sometimes of being a healer and to emphasise that we are regulated by a Code of Conduct and guidelines as other health professionals are. In all my contact with the medical profession over the years I found only a few with closed minds. Some were interested but didn't wish to be seen to be so. I met them mostly in hospitals, when I was called by patients to give treatments there. This was quite acceptable within the NHS as long as the request came from the patients themselves. I of course never agreed to see anyone unless it was by direct request. These hospital visits didn't happen all that often in this area, but usually aroused the curiosity of nurses and doctors, and when time allowed, I would answer their questions. I found hospice doctors and staff particularly interested in healing and I was always warmly welcomed there. Then too, there were a few doctors in my area who openly welcomed the help I could give to their patients, and even encouraged me to continue.

In my first years as a healer people looking for help came to my home. If this wasn't possible I visited them in their homes, sometimes this would be weekly and over long periods of time. In the first year particularly, it seemed that everyone had back injuries, and healing had a high success rate in these cases, particularly if treated immediately after the injury. The number of golfers I saw I am sure was entirely down to my golfing husband Frank! He talked much more openly about my healing than I ever did and he encouraged his friends with back problems to come and see me. Stiff and painful joints were common and difficult to help with healing and always I saw the connection between stiff joints and stiff minds, for these were the people who would come into my home, sit down and announce that no-one could help them. My heart would sink, for initially I found it difficult to get through to people that they could do a great deal to help themselves. Indeed for any recovery to be possible and permanent, it is essential. I said before and I repeat, no recovery can be complete or permanent if we continue to live in the same climate as caused the problem in the first place. Climate in this context refers to personal and home circumstances, work situation and so on, but even more important than any of that is our attitude of mind to these things and to our lives in general. There are no victims in this world, only volunteers. (That statement is explained in the final chapter of the book.)

Some of those who did not view healing as miraculous considered it to be definitely spooky. These people would shy away from the subject and sometimes from me. People shying away from me was obviously not a problem, I had had that when I was little because I was different, but I had to quickly learn how to deal with the ones who told me I was in league with the devil and would end up in hell and other such rubbish! These remarks were usually made by people who considered themselves to be Christians and very sadly I met with them from time to time. One church person

visited me regularly (uninvited of course) to persuade
me to mend my ways and save my soul before it was
too late, as only ordained ministers were allowed to
place hands on anyone for the purpose of healing. It
took great courage in the beginning to stand up and be
counted. It took courage to state in public "I'm a
healer". Frank on the other hand had no hesitation in
saying "My wife is a healer". One of his big
disappointments in life was that I hadn't listened to him
when he urged me to write this book many years ago.
Perhaps having found the courage to write it now will
make up for that, just a little.

There was another occasion when my courage
failed me. I had enrolled as an adult student and where,
when and other details I will not go into, for it is a long
time ago. Initially I got along famously in my chosen
subject, with the other students and with the tutor.
However after a few weeks the tutor discovered I was a
spiritual healer. (The word spiritual has now mostly
been dropped and we are more often referred to as
energy healers. This is more accurate.) Then the attitude
of this tutor to me changed completely and
immediately. Now at every opportunity, I was urged to
give up my ways as I was doing the work of the devil
and all the other usual rubbish. After a time this badly
affected my course work and one day I came to the
conclusion that this harassment just wasn't worth it. I
resigned from the course. My husband was furious with

me for being such a coward and urged me to go back to my studies and report the matter. I now feel ashamed and guilty to admit that even with his support I just could not find that courage. I excused my decision a little by telling myself that perhaps the Universe was whispering to me that maybe this course was not part of my destiny. Certainly I have not missed the qualification in the subject I was studying.

All the healing experience I gained up to this point led to my appointment as a healing tutor around 1996. This was with the Healing Trust, at that time still called The National Federation of Spiritual Healers. I considered this a privilege and I did this for over ten years. Initially three of us taught the courses together. We were limited to ten students for every tutor, but thirty students was quite a handful. These courses attracted nurses, doctors and even a minister on one occasion. He obviously didn't share the opinions of some others I had met! I just loved this teaching, but it was exhausting. Partly this was due to lack of sleep. The energy on these courses reached a very high level indeed, with little privacy or time to unwind. My fellow tutor Rosemary and I shared a room with what turned out to be a handy window and we would be wakened at a very late hour with handfuls of gravel being thrown against our second floor window. After a long training day some of our students liked to relax at a nearby hostelry. (Yes, healers are human too!) They would return after the doors of the centre were locked. We didn't really mind as we were mostly blessed with wonderful dedicated students. Of course healing attracted an oddball or two but that was all part of the challenge of being a tutor. We had a lot of fun on these courses as we both believed that when students are enjoying themselves they learn more, and we always had out third tutor Ian, for a little touch of balance if we needed it!

The healing training was spread over two years and full membership was not possible in under that time. As well as the training courses each student healer had to be mentored for the same period by a full member of the Trust. I willingly did this job too although it took up a lot of time but was so rewarding. Gradually there was a demand for training in different parts of the country, rather than in one central venue, and so I continued teaching healing on my own in my home area.

All through my teaching years with the Trust it fell to me to cover the subject of "Death and Dying". I was more than comfortable with this subject. Of course all our teaching was from the Trust's own teaching notes so that training was standardised across the country, but there was plenty of scope for personal input. For many years now this subject has been so close to my heart and after my husband died when I was 65 my life had to change. I no longer felt that I

175

wanted to see total strangers at any time of day when alone in my home. I passed through a period of great vulnerability. There was a reason for this but more of that later. I was still comfortable seeing people who had been to see me before, but it seemed that without any conscious effort on my part I was now almost only working with the terminally ill. And almost all of them had cancer, as had my husband. I now found myself in the very privileged position of being able to help and support those who had limited time left. This help was not restricted to healing. For instance I was happy to be left in charge of a loved one while a husband or wife took an hour away with complete peace of mind.

Almost everyone facing death wanted my views on life after death. The medical side of dying was not my concern, nor was the accepted religious side of it. It was also not my job to persuade anyone of anything. A fine line had to be drawn, but when asked, and only when asked, for my views on death I simply shared my understanding of the purpose of life, death and the afterlife. Whether anyone believed me or not was also not my problem, but I was more than happy to provide a listening ear if they wished to share their beliefs. During those years I never once entered a single home without being overwhelmingly humbled by the sheer courage and bravery of people facing death.

Lastly with regular healing sessions it was quite amazing how many people lived on, sometimes years, most often months, longer than their doctor's expectations. Always too their quality of life was much better than expected and their final days were peaceful. One person in particular had been given only a few weeks to live when he sought my help. It wasn't his approaching death that troubled him as much as the fact that his wife was totally unprepared and he did not feel she would be able to cope on her own. This man had weekly visits from me and I initially had to overcome his wife's disapproval of this. He spent his extra time (his words) and energy in finding a gardener, installing a watering system for the garden and doing many other things around the home to enable his wife to cope on her own. Finally six months later, when he considered he could do no more, he quietly left this world.

This part of my life, healing into death, lasted for just over ten years when I decided it was the right time for me to allow younger healers to take over. I was and still am so very grateful for this privilege. I refused to charge anyone who was terminally ill, for I didn't want lack of finances to deny anyone of help. Looking back now however, this was probably not the wisest decision I have ever made, for many insisted on giving me vouchers to the equivalent value of my time, and I know they would have much preferred if I had charged. Well, even with the best intentions, we can't always get

177

things right and perhaps I did overlook their feelings a little.

CHAPTER 16

THE UNIVERSE IS WHISPERING TO US

I have always been a bit of a dreamer, and no, I do not mean I live in a make believe world most of the time, I mean I dream a lot in my sleep. If you remember too, I had to pretend that I was having nightmares to explain away my terror when I was going through the phase of having almost nightly visits from groups of or individual spirit people. After that period in my life passed, sadly my untruth turned into reality, no surprises there, and I did indeed start to suffer from periodic nightmares. Some were even repeating ones. We were back to disturbed sleep once again. And again I had no answers. But the answers were there for me to find and this happened in a most unusual way. My husband, Frank, came home one evening and couldn't wait to tell me of a radio programme he had been listening to in his car that morning. This programme took the form of an interview with a lady who had written a book on dream interpretation. It was called *The Dream Book. Symbols for Self-understanding* and the author's name was Betty Bethards. Now I was totally astonished that Frank had even listened to such a programme, far less comment on it. He had no interest in my "weird" studies and anyway while driving, he was strictly a Bach man and eventually even lured me away from Mozart and over to Bach. With my non-musical ear this was probably not very difficult for I doubt that I could identify the music of either accurately. I have no ear for music, but as I discovered on my colour course I can feel it on an emotional level.

But the coincidence Frank said, of my continuing nightmares, and this lady sharing my Christian name, led to him paying attention to what she had to say and he was greatly impressed. So much so that he insisted I get her book because he was convinced that reading it would help me. Now then here I was being given permission to buy another book and head off down another avenue of exploration. How could I resist that? And of course as you can probably guess it didn't stop at one book either.   I love studying and enquiring into all spooky and weird things, as I once considered them to be. Each time I do so I add a few more pieces to my jigsaw, and as Frank said to me on one occasion "What is spooky or weird to others, is just normal in this house". Oh how I liked that!

So what did I find down this new avenue? Well, of course I read all the information on what has been researched about our sleep patterns, the different levels of sleep, such as REM sleep (REM stands for rapid eye movement), and it is during these periods that we actually do our dreaming and so on. This can all be found in any good dream book. I learned quite a lot too about nightmares, and understanding their cause did eventually lead to their disappearance from my life. But what interested me too was reading up on what has been recorded in the past about people using their dreams to enhance their lives. That initially seemed a bit far-fetched to me but I quickly came to see the sense of it and eventually to use it. Many ancient cultures tell of how important the dream-state, as they called it, was in their lives. The Bible tells us of Joseph interpreting his dreams, using the messages contained in them and becoming quite rich by doing so. This hasn't happened to me yet, but maybe I have a little way to go. Joseph too is said to have learned of the danger to baby Jesus in a dream. Now where would we be if he had ignored that one? It seemed that many inventors, writers and others, when they came to a dead end in their conscious thinking, if they then switched off to their problem this allowed their unconscious mind to take over, find the solution and present it to them in the dream-state. Would that we could all have that ability today. This may all seem a bit far-fetched, but just how often have we let go of a problem and then found that the answer dropped into our mind some time later.

I read too, that Coleridge's poem, "Kubla Khan" came to him in a dream (unfortunately unfinished because, although he did dream the whole poem, he was interrupted when writing it down). William Blake is said to have been shown a new method of engraving in a dream. This was copper engraving and he attributed this message to his brother Robert who had died some time before. It was not uncommon it seemed, for music to be heard in dreams and the Italian composer Tartini attributes his piece of music "The Devil's Trill" to a dream. Sir Walter Scott, Keats, Charlotte Bronte to name a few others, acknowledge that their dreams have inspired them. There are many such things documented, including I gather, scientific discoveries and even chemical formulas. The final one I will mention is that in Egypt at the time of the Pharaohs they had dream temples. Anyone could go there to sleep and in the morning there would be skilled dream analysts available to explain the meanings of their dreams. Now I have no means of proving whether these stories are all true or not, and I certainly do not claim that they are, but it does all make interesting reading and suggests that once again we should keep an open mind on this subject as in so many others. And it seems that believing in my dreams shows I am keeping excellent company. I'll settle for that.

It is pretty certain that we all dream whether we remember our dreams or not. These dreams will almost always be in colour but again, we may not remember this. Dreams may last as long as forty minutes or be very short. We seem to remember the dreams we have just before waking much more readily than those that take place earlier in the night. This can be explained by our sleep cycles. I am convinced that some of our dreams are nothing more than a going over of happenings during that day, and these I have learned to recognise and I know I can safely ignore them. Others I just know I have to interpret and take action on if I feel this is called for.

Just as important as our actual dreams are the symbols and pictures that come to us in the hypnagogic state. This state is the few seconds just before falling asleep. I find pictures flash before my eyes and I just know if I have to heed them, but I do find them very hard though to understand. Heeding them is one thing but understanding how to do so is more difficult.

There are many, many books on dream interpretation to buy, or your local library will always carry some or can certainly source them for you. However the most important meaning of any dream or symbol is what it suggests to you personally. I will give you an example of this. If I were to dream of fire, because as a child, we experienced a very serious fire within our home, this dream would almost certainly be warning me to take care in some circumstance around me at the time and the other content of the dream would give me further clues. Someone else who perhaps had only known fire contained within a hearth

183

and maybe even had been in the habit of toasting their toes in front of it, would no doubt regard fire in a dream as something warm and friendly. They would undoubtedly have a good feeling about this dream and they could certainly look forward to something nice happening or perhaps a time of relaxation and comfort. Now I appreciate that this is a very simple comparison but I think it will give you an idea of what I mean about dream meanings and dream dictionaries. Sometimes I have dreams that make little sense to me and this is when a dream dictionary will give me *possible* meanings and I can then usually relate to one of them.

Symbolism is symbolism whether it is presented to us in a dream or in our waking life and we really ought to heed it. Once we start thinking about symbols they can usually be quite easily understood. For instance, in a dream, are you walking on a narrow, rocky, twisting path or a wide smooth straight road? Are you carrying heavy baggage? What does that suggest to you? A path or a road is always our journey through life. Dreaming of houses is interesting because they almost always represent us, spiritual, physical or both. If your dream puts you in the kitchen – check that you are nourishing yourself properly. Clogged pipes in the bathroom – look at your emotions – are you all choked up about something? Anything to do with water suggests the emotions. In your daily life if you have a dripping tap, don't get all fanciful over one tap, get it fixed! But if dripping taps happen a few times, as well as getting them fixed, *that* is the time to do a quick check on your emotions. Do you dream of clutter, untidiness? What is your life like at the moment? Is it time for a bit of a clear out? One of the best books on symbolism that I can recommend is Denise Linn's one titled *Signposts. The Universe is Whispering to you.* This is not an actual dream book, but it is full of *possible* meanings for symbols and is excellent.

Now I know that not all of you will be interested in or even accept that dreams are important, but at least pay attention to the little coincidences and happenings around you, as I know by now you will see how simple it can be to listen to the Universe whispering to us, as Denise puts it.

185

CHAPTER 17

BUT ARE WE ALWAYS LISTENING?

Now I have just given you a wee bit on dreams and symbols because, being who I am, I really do believe in all that stuff, but it would be a good idea if we all also heeded more, what our physical bodies are trying to tell us when we are ill, or even just when under the weather. I don't mean going to bed and resting when we get a bout of 'flu. That surely is just plain common sense. I'm referring to much deeper stuff than that. Certainly the more time I spent healing, the more interested I was to get in this subject, and as I was channelling the healing energy my sensitivity was not only growing in relation to atmospheres, but also to what was going on around each person. I was becoming aware of the deeper reasons for their illnesses.

In particular I was noticing that some people who came for help would sit in my little healing room, and during our preliminary chat, they would tell me just how many doctors, consultants and others had failed to make them well. This statement would be my first clue to possibly why they were ill. They expected someone to wave a magic wand. A skilled surgeon can repair broken bones, remove or replace bits and so on, a doctor can help us with the right drugs, but with more guidance we may be able to work out and identify why our health is giving cause for concern in the first place. Initially I was happy just to channel the energy but now I was no longer content with that. My intuition was prodding me to explore further. I was spurred on in this because of all I had learned about other vibrational medicines, and in particular, by using muscle testing, how our bodies can actually answer our questions. My pendulum works in much the same way.

Now and again I would have a request from a family member for an appointment for a partner or a parent say, but although I had always made the healing energy available to anyone who asked for it, I did insist that the person who needed help be the one to make the request if at all possible. Once or twice a person, usually a man, would come in, sit down and say something like "I must warn you coming to you was not my idea. I don't really want to be here." As if any healer, (let alone an initially reluctant one!) needed that. So if the person concerned made the request this showed at least a degree of willingness to help themselves and hopefully change. However, if that person, even if they recovered completely with healing, continued to live their life exactly as before, making no effort to change in any way, then their illness would return or another one would take its place. We cannot continue to live healthily in the same climate as caused the problem in the first place. Some of you reading this may not want to face that one – but that is how it is and I know I am repeating myself here.

I quickly learned that some complaints or illnesses indicated certain states of mind. I even started my own list of what related to what. For instance when there was stiffness in the body I would most often find that person very difficult to work with. I didn't look forward to their visits for the stiffness in their body usually echoed stiffness in their mind. They were the "always right" people. No-one could help them they would state emphatically. Since we always get what we expect I was often wondering why they had bothered to come to see me at all. Some people can be quite a challenge.

A few people even "enjoyed" ill health. I found this initially a rather strange expression, but I very quickly learned how true it could be. These people really seemed to enjoy talking about their health problems even if others didn't enjoy listening to them. Sometimes their illness was a cop out. Perhaps they had nothing else in their life and it gave them at least a degree of sympathy and attention or just an excuse to opt out of living or making any effort. Often it meant that they didn't have to work. One lady I remember who came for help, had such pain in her shoulder that she was in danger of losing her job. As her husband had been unable to work for some years because of a bad back, she really needed to keep her job in order to build up her pension for her retirement. This might suggest she was "shouldering too much responsibility". With her cooperation and a shifting of how she saw her situation, she made a complete recovery. So why then didn't the husband seek help too? Perhaps he could also have returned to work, but did he want to?

Lower back problems almost always uncovered a degree of worry about finances. I remember one man in particular who had the most dreadful lower back pain. I saw him first in my home, then in his and finally in hospital with little or no betterment until I dug a little deeper and discovered he had recently lost his mother. He had depended on his mother for support all through his life, even after he had married and had a family of his own. This lady was always there underpinning him financially and emotionally. Having lost his "prop", he was then lost and the back pain took over. Sadly healing didn't help much as he just couldn't let go of his worries and nor could he learn to trust in himself and the future. I found this a difficult case to deal with because I knew that he was quite comfortably off financially. I had a lesson to learn here too, it was to know when to let go when I had done all I could.

If you have neck problems, think of what is in your life at this time that you consider is a real pain in the neck. Yes, ok you may decide you have just been sitting in a draught but you still need to look a little deeper. Are you being really stubborn (or stiff necked) about something? Let's look at difficulty in swallowing. This one is very obvious as we even sometimes say that such and such a situation is "hard to swallow".

Look closely at any "accidents" you may have – what was your state of mind when they happened? A good friend and one of my fellow tutors with The Healing Trust, tells an interesting tale. One of her people, a young mum with a very busy life, was having a really bad morning getting her family off to school and work. In desperation she shouted angrily, "Please God, give me a break!" Later that morning she fell and broke her wrist! Could this have been a little lesson on being careful what we ask for? I do think God took her request a bit too literally though! To be serious, we rarely have accidents when we are relaxed and paying attention to what we are doing.

To sum up very briefly, accidents usually indicate anger lurking within us somewhere. Coincidentally while writing this chapter I had a minor but very painful accident. The details are irrelevant but the message was clear. I reluctantly had to admit that deep within I was very angry over a situation in my life, and I didn't feel I could speak up about it. The pain of the accident was slow to clear for I hadn't dealt with the anger, and even when it did, after only a few days it returned quite badly, but this time I found the courage to voice my feelings and in doing so, dissipated my anger and the pain. It didn't have to be like that. I should have known better.

Sore throat and loss of voice – do you need to voice something? Are you denying yourself the right to speak up?

That's enough on this aspect of healing for you to get my message. The more my mind opened to all this, the more clearly I could see possible deeper reasons for illness. Sometimes I only needed to gently bring these possibilities to people's attention, and they were able to make the changes necessary in their lives. Healing of course supported them greatly with this. My list of possible connections between state of mind and body got longer as I gave more and more of my time to it. I even went so far as to start planning a book on this. So what happened? Well, one day I discovered that a very clever lady had got there before me! Her name is Louise L. Hay and she has a number of books to her credit. If you are as fascinated by this aspect of illness as I am, then either her book *"You Can Heal Your Life"* or another one *"Heal Your Body"* will be of great interest to you. The latter is a shortened version of the first. I have other books by Louise Hay too and they have all contributed much to my learning and added quite a number of pieces to my jigsaw. Should you wish to explore this aspect of illness in much greater depth I recommend *The Healing Power of Illness* by Dethlefson and Dahlke. M.D. When I was tutoring in healing and colour this book was a must for me, but I warn you it is quite deep and if you get interested in this aspect of illness you may find out uncomfortable things about yourself. I know I have!

CHAPTER 18

GOD, ARCHANGELS, ANGELS AND SPIRIT PEOPLE

(As I see them)

Having been doing healing work for a long number of years I have spent many hours reading up on spiritual truths written by authors whom I highly respect, and some of whom I have met, or I have been present at and listened to their lectures. As always I have had to sort the wheat from the chaff – *as I see it*. Most of this book can only be written from my own perspective. Parts of it certainly have been proven beyond doubt by scientific research in different countries around the world. But it is only when, in my mind, I have put together all I have learned, that I have come to believe certain things about our world, and other worlds. Since I am still studying and more scientific research is being reported all the time, then who can tell how my beliefs may change in the years to come.   All of this adds up to my knowledge but added to this as I get older, I hope is wisdom. I view "knowledge" as what I have learned and I view "wisdom" as what I have gained through experience. There is a mighty big difference.

193

I did say earlier on that I would try to define later how I view God. Later has arrived, but I must start with the Chapter title in reverse order. After all it was meeting a spirit person all those years ago that started all this off. I used to call spirit people ghosts and some people still do. There is a difference though. If you remember, because of my complete ignorance of the subject, they terrified me at first. There was no shame in that for we don't very often meet spirit people. I now believe that when I die, I too will be a spirit person. I will simply leave my heavy physical body here on earth to be disposed of, and my soul, and this is the real "me", now so much lighter will move on from the physical level into one of the next levels or planes. I do tend to think of this as moving "up" into another level, but I know that there is no "up" for all levels intermingle. This is possible because of the different vibrational frequencies allowing each level to occupy the same space at the same time. That took a whilie for me to understand. Those of my family and friends that I have left on the physical level will not now see me for the very simple reason that I will be vibrating at a different and slightly higher rate. Everything in the whole of the Universe is vibrating energy and there are very many frequencies. We only see what is vibrating at our own rate, and we tend to believe in and be comfortable with only what we can see. But I will still be around. I will not have travelled far. My final absolute proof of this was when my husband, on the day of his funeral, was with me to support me through that day. While I was dressing early in the morning, he spoke to me and made a cheeky remark, and this I heard in my mind loud and clear. This was a very personal remark that only he could have made, and certainly not one that my mind would have thought of, particularly at that time. It was lucky I was alone that morning (my choice may I say) for on "hearing" my husband's words in my head, I collapsed with grief, then laughed at his remark and finally sobbed for a time, ridding my body of much pent up stress, and this undoubtedly helped me get through the rest of that very difficult day.

So assuming I go to the next level, this is called the Astral Plane by the way, I will spend some time there, but after acquiring a bit more learning, I would hope to move into yet another higher vibrational frequency and so on. I believe there are seven levels in all, but each of these levels is divided into many more. I suspect it's going to take me a very long time to get far. I know too that the level we actually go to does depend on what we have done with our lives so far. By that I mean that a very selfish, cruel person will not immediately on death go to the same level as someone who, for instance, has given their life to helping others with no thought of reward. These are extreme comparisons of course. I also believe that the *reason* for doing charity or other work for the good of others is what will count. We still cannot buy our way into Heaven, wherever it is. Heaven to me is more a state of mind than a place. And that should be possible to find here and now.

Now after my death and my consequent change of frequency, those with clairvoyant sight might occasionally see me when conditions are right. I might be able to communicate with them when there is a purpose for doing so, as Frank did with me, and still does now and again when I really need help. I would like to make it clear that I have never heard the "sound" of words. For me it is a mind thing only no matter who is communicating. I have no clairaudient abilities. When I get these messages, they are like no thoughts I have ever had, I just *know* they are from another world. The Astral Plane (this is the next level beyond the one we are on) is the level that the majority of mediums can make contact with, and this was the level my bossy schoolteacher was on. If I ever meet her in the future I will owe her an apology, for I was very rude to her that night so long ago now. This, too, is the level where I may meet my relatives and old friends who died before me and we can have a "catch up". I'm really going to enjoy that. They of course will know all I've been doing, but I will want to hear all their news. I have read that no matter what level a spirit person is on they can change their vibration and come back down to a lower one if there is a purpose for doing so. However it is said that it is not possible to visit higher planes at will, until we have reached a certain level of development. That makes sense to me. Knowing this answers a worrying question I had at one time. It was that as it is now some years since my husband died, would he have moved on to another level by the time I die? I'm much happier knowing that even if he has he will still be there for me. Of course we are also told that only in this physical world is there such a thing as "time". Now with my earthly mind I cannot begin to imagine what it must feel like to live without worrying about time. It seems I will have much to adjust to.

Although I keep using the word "die" you will now understand my total belief that none of us can ever die in *our* dictionary meaning of the word. It is just a moving on process. Believing this removed any fear of dying I may have had, and so very many people that I have discussed this subject with, share this lack of fear of death. But *how* we will die does cross our minds just a little. I do not believe either that I will go to hell for I tend to share Aldous Huxley's suggestion that maybe this world is another Planet's hell.

While I was studying mediumship all those years ago, many times I heard people asking for help through a medium from someone known to them who had passed on. I found this slightly disturbing because it did seem to be a common supposition that those who had

197

died were suddenly a fount of all knowledge and would give expert advice on all problems, including medical matters. I don't think this can be true by a long way. If someone wasn't too knowledgeable while living, they are highly unlikely to know much more immediately after dying and moving up a notch. When they do learn a bit more they too would then move up to yet another level and would not be so easily contacted. It all sounds a bit like school really. I will learn a bit and move on through class after class or, as in this case, level after level, until finally I graduate. The graduation bit is not possible for me to imagine, nor have many people written much about it. Another fallacy, by the way, is that mediums can contact anyone of their choice. I do not believe this to be so either. Every spirit person can choose whether a contact can be made or not, and they will also choose how we or a medium sees them. Very often this is a younger version than that which we remember. Now, if you are uncomfortable about all this stuff please just put it on the back burner until, or if, it feels comfortable to you.

I repeat, mediums can only make contact with a spirit person provided they can achieve the same vibrational frequency as that spirit is on and provided that spirit wishes to be contacted. Do you remember when I started channelling healing energy and I needed to learn this "tuning in" stuff, Bob initially helped me change my physical level frequency to a higher one.

How much we can change our frequency will decide which other planes we can contact. This is what I refer to when I talk of separating the wheat from the chaff. Some mediums, after learning to make contact with the next level, rest on their laurels. Others continue their education and development. It was my experience of "messages" from mediums of this calibre and standing that I came to trust, and those are the ones that I have already spoken of.

Just a word on ghosts and hauntings, these are said to arise when someone dies either very suddenly or perhaps violently and it is difficult for their spirit body to accept that they have actually passed on. That was not the case with my first ghostly encounter in Elgin nor was this so with my "wardrobe folk". They were all trying to make contact with me had I but known it. I have had a few contacts from "lost souls" and I have already told you of those. Another reason for ghosts hanging around is when, for some reason, a soul simply cannot bear to be parted from the place where they lived when alive. With tongue in cheek I ask, is it possible that when ghosts hang around pubs, this may be because they didn't want to give up their favourite tipple? Perhaps I should now move on to the subject of angels!

There is a wealth of books that have been written about angels and archangels. You will find them on the mind, body and spirit shelves in the bookshops, and many more are available on the internet. However I can again only write on this subject as I see it. I have never seen an angel hovering or sitting around in my home or anywhere else. That doesn't mean I don't believe in them or that I am not aware of their presence, because I do and I am. I just don't see them in the way they are portrayed in pictures and probably most of you will be the same.

I have been told that angels are messengers from the highest vibrational level, God, the Creator, the Source or whatever you prefer. Some say that angels have never lived on the earth. Their sole purpose appears to be to help mankind and we are all said to have a special angel and this angel is referred to as our guardian angel. They are said to stay with us through all our lifetimes guiding and helping us when needed but only when we invite them to do so. This is because we all have free will. I am comfortable with all that but what a boring, and stressful job my guardian angel must have had all these years. Now I am aware that I have not told you anything new so far about angels. Although I have said I have never seen one in the accepted form, I will tell you of something that might interest or even intrigue you.

For many years now, ever since I trained in colour with Marie Louise Lacy, I have, at certain times, gone into a room, usually in my own home, and there would be a splodge of colour on a wall or other light coloured surface. Mostly I see these splodges in violet but I have seen other colours as well and they are always clear and bright. Now I am fully aware of afterimages, an afterimage is the true complementary of any colour as I have already explained, and that is not what I am talking about. On consulting with a world famous "angel expert" that I met in Aberdeen, she told me that this is simply another way of seeing angels. These sightings certainly did *always* coincide with important spiritual things happening in my life at the time. I learned too from books, of the names of many of the angels and also of colours associated with them. I also heard of the colour connection while doing my colour therapy training. Am I really seeing angels? I wonder.

During the last few years there has been much written about orbs. These orbs are said to be "angels in disguise". The general explanation seems to be that we and our Planet, are in greater need of help now than ever before in history, (I certainly would agree with that) and this is the reason for the much larger numbers of angels around us. And at times they are showing themselves to us in the form of orbs. These orbs or angels are now being captured by digital photography. The older cameras would not have been able to do this reliably. There are websites displaying, probably hundreds, of photographs of orbs, indoors, outdoors, during the day and at night. They are all there. I had looked at them now and again but kept an open mind. As far as I was concerned the jury was still out.

Then I attended a wedding and later, on receiving copies of some of the photographs taken at the wedding, there on one of them was a clear, perfectly round, transparent orb suspended in the air next to one of the wedding guests. The nearest description I can give is that it was like a really big soap bubble, the kind I blow to entertain my little great grandson. Well, I still didn't know what to make of angel orbs, but decided to sit on the fence a little longer and see if any more proof turned up. And it did.

A fellow healer had dropped by for a catch up on all our latest news one Saturday, and over a cup of tea we were chatting about how much healing he was able to fit in with his work commitments. This appeared to be very little. I was giving him some words of encouragement by saying that when his circumstances changed, and as his family grew up, he would have more time to give to healing and the opportunities would come his way. Then, just touching his right shoulder there appeared the most beautiful orb and while I sat gazing in awe, a second one, slightly smaller and just above and a little to the right of the first orb slowly took form. They stayed there for a good few minutes before fading out. Well make of all that what you will, but I am now pretty convinced. I must add too that at no time had this healing friend and I ever discussed orbs. When I told him of what I was seeing he said that he had actually never even heard of them.

Archangels come next and I believe they have more wisdom than angels and that they too work for the benefit of, not only our Planet, but the whole of the Universe. They are said to each have special areas of expertise and if we ask them, they too will help us. I did read once that Archangel Michael was said to have an affinity with computers for instance. And before you ask, no I have never appealed to an Archangel when I can't get on to the internet. I usually take rather more down to earth measures.

And finally for this chapter we come to God, the Source, the Creator, All That Is. Is God a He or a She? Who can say? So how do *I* view God? To be honest this is not a subject that I have given a great deal of thought to, until I came to write this chapter. Before I started on my journey of discovery the Christian definition of God was all I knew and I am still very comfortable using the word "God". But now with much greater understanding I would take you back to all that I have already said about the "energy" that is all around us and available to us all, provided we can tune in to the right wavelength. The Source of this energy I believe to be what others call God.

This same energy I believe can be used to create anything in our lives, hence another name for God – the Creator. I believe we all (and every other thing upon this earth) originate from and are part of this energy and therefore we are all part of God and connected to each other. That was the message that came over so strongly for me during the meditation when I was in Chicago. Remember it? "What we do unto others, we do unto ourselves". It could not be clearer or simpler.

On the other hand, in my day to day life, when my birds flock to my garden to be fed in the morning, it is God I thank for their presence and for brightening my day. When the beauty of the flowers in my garden overwhelm me, it is to God I send my gratitude. When an animal chooses my knee to sit upon I thank God for its love and trust. When my heart is full of joy I acknowledge Him as its Source. Need I say any more?

CHAPTER 19

I AM WHO I WAS BORN TO BE

I did not intend writing this last chapter. I am doing so by special request. It seems that it is of interest to some of those who have read my first book, "The Crofter Quine". Specifically I was asked to put down on paper how being born illegitimate had influenced or affected the rest of my life. I do know from having done quite a number of book talks, just how many people share my story to some extent, if not all of it. I have been told over and over how much hearing of my experiences had put their own more into perspective. That worked both ways, for they in turn by sharing a little of their feelings, helped me too. Standing out in my memory are one or two people who were obviously very emotionally affected during the talks, and at the end of the evenings they approached me and shared in a whisper that their situations at birth and even later had almost exactly matched my own. Some of them would then go on to say that because of the shame of this, they had never once up to that evening when they approached me, talked about it, and even in some cases their own family did not know of their illegitimacy. Now just how heart-rending is that? I can so well understand though how they felt. Back in the early 1930's the shame of such a start in life was great. So much so that when my boyfriend Frank asked me to marry him I felt before I answered, I had to ask him "Do you realise I am illegitimate?" Now it didn't matter one scrap to Frank, but subsequently I learned just how much it mattered to his parents. And how sad was that too. So if my story helps even one other person then this book will have been worthwhile. I am well aware of the massive shift in thinking and behaviour since then, but perhaps now the pendulum has swung a little too far the other way. Only time will tell if this is true.

The title of this chapter came to me at 6a.m. one morning (the best time for thinking by the way) and of course it is from Susan Boyle's song. I cry a little every time I hear it – not ever tears of sadness – always tears of joy, of gratitude for all I had and still have, pride in my family and I suppose just a little too in what I have been able to make of my life so far, for I believe that I alone am responsible for what I have made of the hand I was dealt at birth. After all I firmly believe that I chose that hand, and what I have made of it is controlled completely by what I think and believe. Remember too though, that all I now know came to me only gradually over the years and would not have done so had my mind not been, at times so reluctantly, receptive to it.

Since the publication of my first book I have been truly astonished to find that some people consider that the start I had in this life was a bit of a raw deal. Very briefly for new readers, I said I was born illegitimate in the early 1930's – not a good thing to happen to you at that time. During my early years at school I was, let's just say "avoided", but it was a bit worse than that, because of this "accident" of birth. At the time and for some years at school I just learned to live with it accepting that I was "different", but never really knowing why because any questions I asked were always angrily dismissed.

I had been fostered immediately after birth for about a year, then advertised and finally adopted by the Smith family. As was common at that time a sizeable sum of money was paid to them. The Smiths were cottars, farm servants in other words, and this money enabled them to leave this life behind and find a better way to live. A fair exchange I would say, even if it did leave me with none of the mother/baby bonding that is now considered so important.

Life on crofts at that time was hard with everyone doing their share of the work. That was mostly Mum, Dad and me, as my brothers were in the Forces during the Second World War and at that time, to make ends meet my Dad had to have a full time job as crofts were barely profitable. *But* the Smiths now owned their own land. Today with so many people owning their own homes you cannot begin to imagine how important that was and I am proud to have been, even in a small part, instrumental in my family achieving this, and there is no doubt in my mind that the Smith family is *my* family.

Now how did these "humble origins", as it was described to me on one occasion, affect me in later life? To explain that I must ask you to take a close look at the people in my life and the circumstances of it. My birth mother, Beatrice Ritchie, was living in Aberdeen and was only 18 years old when she found herself pregnant. My father was the son of the house where she worked as a domestic servant. The money paid over on my adoption was provided by my paternal grandmother. I can readily understand my mother's actions at that time. Many years on she told me that all she could think of was how to get rid of me and get on with her own life. Harsh words indeed but who has the right to judge her?

Then the story gets interesting. My mother left Aberdeen and moved to Glasgow where no one would know of her past. While there she worked in a dress shop, and as a wardrobe mistress at one of the theatres. She saved hard and sailed off to the World Trade Fair in New York with a very large empty suitcase. Now how was that for courage? I have inherited some of her courage, but have used it in an entirely different way. Apart from anything else I am not a good traveller, I need to adjust my thinking to that one, but I am working on it. I can at least now get to the Borders without feeling homesick. Big deal I hear you say. At the Trade Fair my mother purchased from her savings as many ladies' garments, (I think they were mostly dresses) as she could afford and returned to Glasgow. These dresses of course came from the famous fashion houses of the time. She then unpicked them and made her own patterns from them, no doubt altering them here and there. These patterns were then used by her to make replica garments and these she sold to the wealthy ladies in Glasgow. The connections here were made through the store where she had previously worked. She also made use of her other connections to the actresses who played the Glasgow theatres. Ignoring how this might breach copyright laws today, I am stunned at her courage, talent, ingenuity and vision. I am proud to say that to some extent I did inherit her stitching skills, the rest of what she achieved would have been quite beyond me for not only am I a poor traveller, selling anything I have made is also not one of my strengths. I have got better at it as I get older, but not a lot.

Having got to know many of the theatrical stars of the time my mother, also called Betty by the way, married and she and her husband bought, first the Gleneagles Hotel in Torquay and later another one over the road. Her contacts with the actors and actresses at

209

that time no doubt helped business greatly. Later, after John Cleese and others stayed at the Gleneagles Hotel in Torquay it became the model for the "Faulty Towers" series on television and the character of Sybil Faulty was "loosely based" on my mother. Or so I have been told. I will say no more on that!

I am also told I have inherited my mother's love of gardening and flowers. I have already told you that at one point in my life I had three gardens, a small dried flower arranging business and of teaching flower arranging for some years. I also inherited my mother's love of embroidery and again I have told of having a professional qualification in this, teaching it for very many years and recently I held my own exhibition. And that is apart from making my own and all my daughter's clothes for many years, even when I didn't own a sewing machine. I would like to add that hand stitching clothes is an occupation I do not wish to revive and anyway my dressmaking skills pale in comparison to that of my mother. I think though I have the edge on her with my embroidery skills.

My half-sisters tell me that I share her mannerisms, particularly the use of my hands when talking, something I was unaware of until it was pointed out to me. I also apparently share her turn of phrase, even down to using some of the same words. Now isn't that all weird when I only spent a few hours with her when I was about three years old and she came to see me, and another few hours one day when I was sixty eight and she was eighty six. She told me then that all her life she had put her energy into her passion for money. Would she have had this passion for money had she not been left penniless and "holding the baby" as a teenager, I ask? I thanked her then for sharing that passion with me but explained that I have used that same energy or passion in a totally different way. This did not impress her greatly. Sadly that second day spent with her was not one I care to remember in detail or to share, but I stand by what I said then. I respect the decision she made after my birth, and her right to make it. Who among us has the right to judge another? And who would not be profoundly grateful for all the skills that I inherited from her?

Now I am aware that my attitude to all of what I have told you may differ from that of some of you, and so perhaps this is a good time for me to repeat some of, and to give you a fuller explanation of how I view the reincarnation stuff I spoke of earlier. Prepare to be surprised, but stick with me, it may just all be true! Not only do I believe that I have lived on this earth many times, I also believe that before each of those lifetimes I have been given the opportunity to choose what I wish to learn from each particular life on earth. I also choose where I will be born and almost certainly I will choose my parents and circumstances of birth. Now do you see where I am coming from? I *chose* the circumstances of my birth and I consider I was very lucky to have found anyone to live through what my birth mother did, giving me the opportunity to experience abandonment, for I also believe that was part of my learning this time round. And yes, that has hurt all these years, at times to the point of being unbearable, but I have learned to accept it and be grateful for the rest. I do not believe there are any victims in this world. By choosing the circumstances of my present life I can only regard myself as a volunteer.

Now we come to the Smiths. I must have had a pre-birth contract with them too. I believe they were always meant to be the ones to bring me up. I suspect Mum Smith found it very hard to keep that contract, and had she been aware that on another level, she had actually agreed to it, she may have regretted that decision. But there it was. As neither Mum nor Dad had a great deal of education, definitely not their fault, my education took a bit of a back seat when it came to a choice between what needed to be done on the croft and my studies. I have no hard feelings and no regrets on that score. It was never meant to be, and I doubt that I would have made a brilliant scholar anyway. The university of life has suited me just fine. I am very much a creative right brained person and living on a croft with a war on, I was in an ideal place to develop the creative qualities inherited from my birth mother. What I am most grateful to Mum Smith for was teaching me to share, share and share. She would have given a stranger her last penny, as that old saying goes.

For instance, during the war years she shared our weekly meat ration with a family on a low income. As she halved our already meagre portion of meat she would say, "We can always eat an egg, they can't". At the time I didn't always share her sentiments. Shame on me! And also, soldiers on exercise near the croft came regularly to our house asking if we had any food to spare. They never left empty handed as my Mum trusted completely that if she helped these poor soldiers, someone would care for her laddies wherever they were. From the tales my brothers brought home after the war had ended, it was obvious that Mum's trust was misplaced, but who can but admire her for it. And how could I have had a better role model? My birth mother certainly could not have provided that.

Yes, there were very bad times in my life at that time. Our family now believe that Mum developed the early stages of dementia at a relatively young age. Even if she had seen a doctor we doubt that, back then, this would have been diagnosed. Remember too doctors at that time had to be paid, a very sound reason for avoiding them, for money was always scarce on a croft. These years have left some scars, a fear of not being able to look after myself as I get older for instance. This probably stems from the empty threats Mum made during her bad times. But on the other hand, this "fear" has led me to develop a fiercely independent nature. This is my description by the way – others may describe it as sheer bloody-mindedness when it comes to accepting help. (There and I thought I didn't know any long words!) So, on a lighter note, every negative has a positive, that is universal law.

Now I come to my Dad. What did I learn from him? We'll not go into how he taught me to drive an old metal wheeled tractor before I was tall enough to reach the pedals when sitting, even when he had never driven one himself! I found it hard to forgive that deception, or how to feed the sheaves of oats into a threshing mill, fifty feet off the ground when I was about eleven. (I exaggerate a little here, but not a lot.) I must be serious for a minute. Although my mind is now full of all these modern beliefs and sayings such as "You can if you think you can", this all started really with my Dad. He allowed and encouraged me from an early age to climb any molehills that got in my way, and you see, this meant that the mountains I was faced with later in life held no fears for me. Nothing, but nothing ever stopped him doing what he set out to do. If we needed a henhouse say, he would make a henhouse. It might not be beautiful, or a something to be proud of henhouse, but it would serve the purpose and who said all henhouses had to be beautiful anyway? "It'll serve the purpose" was one of his favourite sentences. A last resort would be parting with money for some necessity and that would usually be second hand from a roup. It would take "a big think" (another one of his expressions) before he would buy new from a shop. But, can you see, having a Dad like that, meant that he was perfectly happy when I didn't quite get things perfect, I quickly learned that to do my best was fine. And God never asks any more of us anyway. Who would have changed a Dad like that? I consider I was greatly blessed to have had those three parents.

All other hang ups I may have had or have are of little importance when I believe that I am always in the right place at the right time for my soul's development. And yes, I was born to be different, but so was every other person on this planet. I thank God every day because I know, "I am who I was born to be".

Betty Fotheringham

Made in the USA
Charleston, SC
18 September 2014